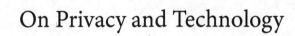

On Privacy and Technology

On Privacy and Technology

DANIEL J. SOLOVE

OXFORD
UNIVERSITY PRESS

OXFORD
UNIVERSITY PRESS

Oxford University Press is a department of the University of Oxford.
It furthers the University's objective of excellence in research, scholarship,
and education by publishing worldwide. Oxford is a registered trade mark of
Oxford University Press in the UK and in certain other countries.

Published in the United States of America by Oxford University Press
198 Madison Avenue, New York, NY 10016, United States of America.

Library of Congress Cataloging-in-Publication Data
Names: Solove, Daniel J., 1972– author.
Title: On privacy and technology / Daniel J. Solove.
Description: New York : OUP, 2025. | Includes index. |
Identifiers: LCCN 2024042708 (print) | LCCN 2024042709 (ebook) |
ISBN 9780197771686 (hardback) | ISBN 9780197771693 |
ISBN 9780197771709 (epub) | ISBN 9780197771716
Subjects: LCSH: Privacy, Right of. | Technology and law. |
Technological innovations—Law and legislation. |
Information technology—Law and legislation.
Classification: LCC K3264.C65 S659 2025 (print) | LCC K3264.C65 (ebook) |
DDC 342.08/58—dc23/eng/20240911
LC record available at https://lccn.loc.gov/2024042708
LC ebook record available at https://lccn.loc.gov/2024042709

DOI: 10.1093/9780197771716.001.0001

Printed by Marquis, Canada

In memory of Michael Sullivan (1966–2022)

Mike was my best friend in law school. A brilliant thinker and the most erudite person I've known, Mike would go on to become a philosophy professor at Emory University. While we were both law students, Mike and I had countless conversations from which I learned an immeasurable amount of philosophy. Mike has had a lasting influence on me. I was fortunate to have some great teachers, but of all of them, Mike was the best.

Contents

Preface   x

PART I HOW TO THINK ABOUT PRIVACY AND TECHNOLOGY

What is Privacy?   3

What is Technology?   6

Why is Privacy Important?   8
  The Social Value of Privacy   8
  The Nothing-to-Hide Argument   9
  Privacy's Role in Individual Life and Societal Structure   10

Framing and Metaphors   14
  Framing Effects   14
  The Physicality of Machines and Data   15
  Humans in the Machine, Humans in the Data   16
  Metaphors for Understanding Privacy Problems   17

Myths   20
  The Myth of the Privacy Paradox   20
  The Myth of Technology Exceptionalism   21
  The Myth That Regulation Stifles Innovation   21
  The Myth That Changes in Degree Don't Matter   22
  The Myth That the Law Is an Interloper   23
  The Myth of Technology Neutrality   24

PART II DIMENSIONS OF TECHNOLOGICAL CHANGE

Information and Knowledge   29
  Flow   29
  Memory   31
  Obscurity   33
  Aggregation   36
  Inference   37

Judgments and Decisions   40
  Prediction   40
  Automation   43
  Reputation   46
  Consent   48

Thought and Behavior   53
  Expectation   53
  Design   55
  Distance   58
  Manipulation   60
  Relationships   61

Power   66
  Control   66
  Inequality   68
  Identification   70
  Cost   72
  Scale   74
  Harm   75
  Vulnerability   77
  Accountability   79

PART III POWER, LAW, AND ACCOUNTABILITY

Privacy and Power   85

The Law's Role   87
  The Canard of Self-Regulation   87
  The Impossibility of Self-Help   88

The Futility of Individual Control 89
The Failure of Privacy Self-Management 90
Privacy and Milk 91

How the Law Should Develop 94
The Virtues of Open-Ended Laws 94
Reframing for a Broader View 95
The Danger of Ossification 97
Privacy Is Complicated, But the Law Is Too Simple 99
Making Enforcement Meaningful 101
The Virtues of a Case-by-Case Approach 102
The Virtues of a Polycentric Approach 103
The Humanities Are Essential 104

A Bolder Path for Law 105

Acknowledgments 110
About the Author 111
Notes 112
Index 122

Preface

This book is about how technology is changing privacy. I have been writing about this issue for about twenty-five years, and I wrote this book to synthesize my thinking in a succinct and accessible way.

Although technology poses grave threats to privacy, technology per se isn't the enemy. I love technology. In the 1980s, when I was twelve, my mom bought an Apple IIe computer. Burned out from her career as a nursing-home administrator, she decided to go back to college to take classes in computer science because she had heard that computers were the "wave of the future." With 64K of RAM, a slow, whirring floppy-disk drive, and a green-screen monitor, the computer was primitive, but I was mesmerized by this magical machine, a portal to endless possibilities and infinite wonder.

Technology can be luminous—but, like the sun, too much exposure to it without thoughtful precautions can singe in the short term and be lethal in the long term.

If there's a villain in the story, it is the law's role as well as certain ways of thinking about technology, privacy, and the law.

I've been on a long intellectual journey into privacy law, shaped by companions along the way and voices from the past. Ideas and perspectives from many different fields have had a lasting impact.

My initial interest in privacy was sparked when taking Professor Jack Balkin's cyberspace-law course at Yale Law School in 1996. It was the first time he had taught it. Though hardly any internet cases had been decided at the time, Balkin conducted his class with great wit, depth, and theoretical insight. Though it was still unclear whether the internet would become a "thing," we had a sense that it would be transformative.

I became immersed in the internet. Ironically, I initially used it to hunt for physical books, objects whose continued existence the digital revolution is now threatening. I love books made of paper—their smell, their texture, their weight. I love collecting them and organizing them, searching for them on shelves, holding them and browsing through them. In the mid-1990s, before the internet had turned into the enemy of books, it enabled me to obtain nearly any volume I wanted. One of the first books I bought online was Alan Westin's *Privacy and Freedom* (1967), an early book about privacy in the Digital Age which was out of print at the time.

I already knew I wanted to be a law professor. I hoped to incorporate humanities thinking into my scholarship, but I lacked a suitable legal topic to explore. After Balkin's class, I decided that I'd write on cyberspace law and bring a humanities perspective to law-and-technology issues. The work of Richard Weisberg and James Boyd White showed me that literature—my favorite source for understanding this bewildering world—could provide productive insights for legal thought. I was also inspired by Martha Nussbaum's eloquent *Poetic Justice* (1995), where she extols the "literary imagination" as an important dimension of rational argument.

In 1997, as I was finishing law school, I began working on my first law-review article about privacy. In preparation, I read everything published about privacy, which was easy at the time because not much had been written. At the time I thought I'd be a cyberlaw scholar in a general sense, and that I'd write just a few pieces about privacy before moving on to other issues. But I discovered that I had gone down a rabbit hole; privacy turned out to be a far larger topic than I had imagined, almost boundlessly vast. No matter how far I journeyed, the terrain kept stretching out before me. And my exploration continues to this day.

My work owes a great debt to John Dewey, who so deftly fused theory and practice, humanities and science, breaking the barriers between siloed subject areas. His thought remains immensely productive and empowering. Philosophies can be analogized to rooms to live in: some are uncomfortable, some are spacious, some are cramped. Dewey's is capacious and lively. Although pragmatism is heavily methodological, its method and ways of thinking are based on commitments to open-minded inquiry, intellectual exploration, and constant interrogation of one's settled views.[1] Dewey's philosophy brilliantly integrates science, technology, and the humanities. He remains relevant—and I'd even say *vital*—to the contemporary Digital Age, and he should be read more widely today.

In this book, I aim to provide a succinct overview of my thinking about privacy over the past twenty-five years. I endeavor to catalog the ways technology is changing privacy and why these changes matter, and I discuss the law's role in responding to these changes. How we understand the relationship between law, technology, and privacy is essential to whether we can successfully protect privacy in our world of rapidly evolving technologies.

Washington,
DC 2024

PART I

HOW TO THINK ABOUT PRIVACY AND TECHNOLOGY

How is technology changing privacy?
Are we doomed?
Is there anything we can do?

"Privacy is dead!" This cry has rung out again and again as we have witnessed the rapid rise of new digital technologies: wiretapping, surveillance cameras, smartphones, the internet, algorithms, artificial intelligence, machine learning, facial recognition, biometric identification, smart devices, social media, heat sensors, drones, behavioral advertising, targeted marketing, and more. With every new advance in technology, the obituaries for privacy pour in. Yet, despite the dire declarations across decades, privacy—though wounded and weary—somehow stumbles on. Can privacy be saved? What should be done?

Technology advances like a relentless army, nearly impossible to halt. Meanwhile, policymakers have desperately been trying to protect privacy by passing countless privacy laws. In the United States, many federal and state laws have been enacted to protect privacy, though most of them are anemic. In the European Union, the General Data Protection Regulation (GDPR) of 2016 represents a grand achievement—the best privacy law in the world—though along with its great features it also has many flaws and falls far short of what is needed. Many privacy laws enacted around the world have been modeled on the GDPR but are typically weaker.

The laws generally have a common set of problems. They place too much of the onus for managing privacy on individuals who lack the time and expertise to do so. They fail to sufficiently address issues of power and the structure of the data ecosystem. They often fail to hold creators and users of technology accountable. They fail to create the right incentives to lead to ethical and responsible behavior. They mandate requirements that end up being performed in a perfunctory manner, often as mere exercises in paper pushing.[1] And they often lack rigorous and comprehensive enforcement, thus ending up as little more than hollow statements of principle.

Overall, while some laws have moved the needle a few notches, their impact overall has been modest. Technology's assault on privacy continues apace. New digital technologies are developing exponentially. More personal data is being collected at every instant; surveillance is enveloping nearly every corner of the world; and our data is being used in a myriad of ways that have profound effects on our lives.[2]

Are we doomed to watch helplessly as technology turns our world into a terrible blend of Franz Kafka's *The Trial*, George Orwell's *1984*, Aldous Huxley's *Brave New World*, and Margaret Atwood's *The Handmaid's Tale*? Can anything be done to save us from a dystopian world without privacy?

Addressing technology's assault on privacy is a formidable task, but there nevertheless are things that the law can do. In order to respond to the challenges that technology poses for privacy, we must first have an understanding of what is happening and why.

What is Privacy?

Privacy is a concept of bewildering complexity. Ceaseless attempts have been made to define the term, but they all have failed. Many attempts at defining privacy have been too broad, making them so vague and all-encompassing that they become rather useless. Other conceptions have been too narrow, excluding elements that ought to be included. Nevertheless, conceptualizing privacy continues to matter, because it affects the scope of privacy laws and determines what is protected and what isn't.

I struggled with conceptualizing privacy for a long time before I discovered a way out—the problem is with the method. A traditional method for defining concepts is to look for a common denominator for all things to be included. But privacy is too dynamic, contextual, and elusive to be pinned down. Instead, the concept of privacy should rely on Ludwig Wittgenstein's "family resemblance" approach to definition. In *Philosophical Investigations*, Wittgenstein argued that some concepts do not have "one thing in common" but "are *related* to one another in many different ways."[1] Applying Wittgenstein's insight to privacy, we should conceptualize privacy as not just one thing but many different yet related things.[2] There is no common denominator to all things under the rubric of "privacy"; instead, these things are related to each other but in different ways.

Privacy is the protection against certain forms of societal impingement on individuals that affect their personal life. The best way to understand privacy is to focus on the activities that can cause disruptions to personal life that might require interventions. To flesh out the web of different things that constitute privacy, I have advanced a taxonomy of privacy that includes four general categories and sixteen subcategories of activities that can lead to disruptions of private life. The general categories are (1) *information collection*, the methods by which data about people is collected; (2) *information processing*, the storage, use, and analysis of personal data; (3) *information dissemination*, the means by which personal data is transferred or disclosed; and (4) *invasions*, direct interferences with an individual's life. Protecting privacy involves addressing all these issues.[3]

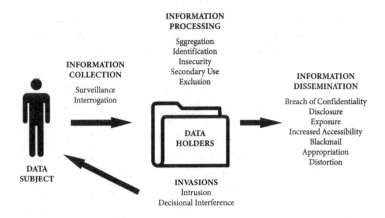

I began developing the taxonomy about two decades ago through a bottom-up approach, using historical, sociological, literary, legal, philosophical, and other sources from the humanities. (I won't go into detail about the subcategories here. If you want to learn more, my book *Understanding Privacy* describes each of them.)

When I originally developed the taxonomy, I noted that it was envisioned as a living project, not the final word on the subject. As time and technology have marched on, new problems have emerged, some of which were best dealt with by adding new subcategories to the general categories. In the future, I will likely revisit and update the taxonomy; many years of studying privacy and following the manifold developments in technology have enriched and deepened my understanding. But I don't anticipate making radical changes, as I think the taxonomy mostly holds up.

Privacy must be freed from the tyranny of myopic definitions. If it is conceptualized too narrowly, then many privacy considerations won't be weighed properly against competing considerations, and many problems that fall outside of crabbed conceptions of privacy will remain unaddressed. Ultimately, privacy involves a broad landscape of problems, and we should think about privacy expansively.

What is Technology?

"The fire stolen from the gods will light men their way
even while it burns their hands." — Zia Haider Rahman[1]

Technology, an immensely broad term, denotes the practical application of knowledge. Technology involves methods and processes for doing things more efficiently. Technology has given us the basic building blocks of modern civilization—energy, agriculture, urbanization, and sanitation—and more. These days, many of the most prominent technological advances relate to digital technologies involving personal data. When I speak about technology in this book, I will be referring to such digital technologies.

Technology involves inventing tools to carry out tasks faster, cheaper, bigger, and better. Although many technology developers aspire to improve the world, the outcome of their work always turns out to be more complicated and ambiguous—often a mixture of gain and loss, delight and danger. The industrial revolution set us on a path to traverse the globe, fly the skies, go to the moon, and communicate worldwide in an instant—and also on a path toward potentially annihilating most of the life on the planet. From one perspective, the story of the industrial revolution and what has followed it can be seen as a victory. At the outset, factories were belching out pollution and workers were brutally exploited, but the law has wrestled with these problems with considerable success. With technology, we have tamed the natural world, lengthened human life, combated disease, and freed ourselves significantly from countless perils and discomforts that nature has thrown in our path.

In many ways, this has been a success story. But from another perspective, the story appears to be heading toward a hideous end—the ruin of the world through climate change. Despite our progress, efforts to control the changes wrought by technology might fall short and lead to our doom.

The story of privacy and technology is one of seduction. Technology beguiles and dazzles us, offering convenience, speed, power, and even beauty. The internet shimmers with delights, a garden of endless possibilities. But the garden turns out to be filled with vipers. Like Odysseus's crew, we eagerly devour Circe's food and drink her wine; we know the fate that awaits us but we can't stop—the food is simply too delicious, the wine too intoxicating. The technologies that allow us to communicate around the world, to carry a computer in our pockets, and to analyze massive quantities of data in a nanosecond seem to be leading simultaneously to a utopia and a dystopia.

We can't abstain from technology, and we shouldn't. Technology has provided wondrous advances and solved intractable problems.[2] Life wouldn't be better without technology; it would be nasty, brutish, and short. Nature isn't designed for our comfort or flourishing; it is something to be survived. And through technology, humans have not only survived but thrived. Art, culture, and philosophy are all possible because technology has freed us from the constant burden of battling with nature.

Technology isn't evil, but it is powerful and transformative. The digital technologies of our times are posing profound challenges for privacy, and we must act urgently. But the law isn't responding in the right ways—and it often is making the problems worse.

Why is Privacy Important?

Technology is affecting privacy today in profound ways, with implications that reverberate throughout society, impacting not just individuals but the entire social fabric. To understand what is at stake, it is essential to understand value of privacy.[1]

The Social Value of Privacy

Privacy is often thought of as an individual interest.[2] Because of this widespread perception, privacy tends to fare poorly in policymaking decisions when it clashes with other interests defined in terms of social value, such as free speech, security, innovation, efficiency, and transparency.[3] When pitted against such ideals, protecting the rights of lone individuals rarely wins.

But viewing the value of privacy as an individual interest is reductive and incomplete, since privacy is also a social value, in at least two ways: (1) It protects individuals for the sake of the greater social good, and (2) it helps construct societal frameworks that distribute power more fairly and productively. As John Dewey aptly observed, individuals and society are intertwined and inseparable: "We cannot think of ourselves save as to some extent *social* beings. Hence we cannot separate the idea of ourselves and our own good from our idea of others and of their good."[4] Individuals and society are interdependent. Individuals are born into society, raised by members of society, educated by society, and shaped in every way by society; society, in turn, grows and improves through countless individual contributions.

Dewey's view of the individual and society remains consistent with robust protection for individual freedom; however, his justification for that freedom is based on protecting individuals not for their own sake but because doing so benefits society. Protecting individual privacy makes society a better environment, fostering creativity, happiness, intellectual exploration, and the ability to realize one's potential— all of which, in turn, further benefit society by facilitating greater contributions to the common good.

When understood as a social value, privacy shouldn't readily suffer by comparison with other ends that are often defined in terms of their social value. The principle of free speech, for example, can be conceptualized broadly as a social value, safeguarding the speech of everyone, rather than narrowly, protecting one individual's speech in a particular case. Though the speech in question in a particular free speech case may not be of profound importance, the ideal of free speech as elevated to the societal level has great power. We protect individual speech— even when it is crass, stupid, or trivial—because we value the freedom to speak as a general principle, as an essential foundation for a free and democratic society. The same holds true for privacy.[5]

The Nothing-to-Hide Argument

I have constantly heard people say that the government should be allowed to engage in unchecked and limitless surveillance. "Why should I care about privacy? I've got nothing to hide," they proclaim. "Only if you have something to hide should you have something to fear."[6]

Responses to such nothing-to-hide arguments often point out things that people might indeed want to hide, such as naked photos. But these responses cede too much ground, since the nothing-to-hide argument is flawed at its foundation. It assumes that privacy is about protecting particular individuals who want to conceal illegal and immoral things. But this is a reductive way to conceive of privacy. Privacy concerns a plurality of related interests that are valuable for promoting the social good. In order to engage in activities that may be unpopular or controversial, people need freedom from government surveillance. Privacy also protects against abuses of government power. The playbook for tyranny is filled with pages devoted to diminishing the privacy of citizens through massive data gathering and surveillance. This is why protecting privacy is about much more than hiding things: it represents the preservation of a zone of freedom essential for creativity, expression, and innovation, and a bulwark against excessive power.

Characterizing privacy in the limited individualistic terms of the nothing-to-hide argument skews attempts to balance privacy and security in policymaking debates. Too often, security is cast as a social value and privacy is sacrificed at its altar. Even worse, many sacrifices of privacy in the name of security have mainly served as what could be called "security theater"—providing a fictitious illusion of safety rather than substantive protection.[7]

Good policymaking depends upon a comprehensive conception of privacy, not a narrow view that minimizes its weight when balanced against conflicting interests.

Privacy's Role in Individual Life and Societal Structure

There are many ways in which privacy plays an essential role in personal life and society. I will discuss some of its most important roles below.

Limit on Power

Privacy represents a limit on the power of the government and companies. Personal data can be used to shape decisions and influence behavior. In the wrong hands, it can be used to cause great harm. History is rife with examples of governments and companies using personal data to attack and discredit people, to discriminate against people, to wrongly detain and eliminate people, and to engage in oppressive social control.

Respect for Individuals

Respecting a person's privacy is essential for respecting their personhood, and ignoring a person's reasonable desire for privacy without a compelling purpose is disrespectful or worse. Though the desire for privacy can conflict with other key values against which privacy will not always win out, a basic respect for personal agency dictates that a person's desire for privacy should always be recognized and acknowledged.

Reputation Management

Privacy provides people with the ability to manage their reputations. Reputation can affect career opportunities, friendships, and overall well-being. Although complete control over one's reputation is impossible, it is important that people be able to protect themselves from being unfairly tarnished. And there are legitimate reasons to protect people not only from falsehoods but also from the disclosure of certain truths. Knowing more private details about people doesn't necessarily lead to better judgment of their character. Judgments about others are often made hastily based on incomplete information. Because we rarely know the complete story about another person, privacy shields information that can too readily be misconstrued.

Maintaining Appropriate Social Boundaries

People establish physical and informational boundaries around themselves. In order to relax, to be candid and at ease, people need situations of solitude and retreat where they can escape the gaze of others. People establish informational boundaries that vary across different relationships, and privacy is an essential aspect of these boundaries. Since breaches of such boundaries can lead to awkward social interactions and damage relationships, privacy also serves to reduce social friction. Most people don't want everybody to know everything about themselves—hence the phrase "None of your business." And most people actually don't want to know everything about others, either—hence the phrase "Too much information."

Trust

All relationships depend upon trust, which is vital not only in dealings with lawyers, doctors, and other professionals but also in our personal and commercial relationships. A breach of confidentiality is a breach of trust, and a breach of trust in one relationship can cause people to lose faith in other relationships. Since our relationships represent crucial strands in the fabric of society, they must be protected.[8]

Fair Decisions About One's Life

Personal data is a core component of many decisions affecting people's lives. It may be critical for receiving a loan or being hired for a job. It is used by the government to determine whether individuals will be investigated or denied the ability to fly. Indeed, personal data affects nearly all aspects of life. People are helpless if they don't have a say in how their personal data is used or the ability to have awareness and input in decisions affecting them.

Freedom of Thought and Speech

Privacy is essential for intellectual freedom, including freedom of speech, freedom of belief, and freedom in the consumption of ideas.[9] Watchful eyes can chill our exploration and expression of information and opinion. Privacy is also key to protecting the communication of unpopular messages. Privacy protects not only fringe activities but also conventional interactions such as speaking candidly with friends, family, or colleagues.

Freedom of Social and Political Activities

Privacy is key to protecting our ability to engage politically. We protect the privacy of voting to ensure that citizens vote based on their true opinions. The privacy of political activities apart from actual voting is important, too. Individuals should be able to engage in policy discourse freely with people they trust without worrying about the watchful gaze or the intrusive ear.

Ability to Change and Have Second Chances

People change throughout their lives, and they need opportunities to have a second chance, move beyond past mistakes, and reinvent themselves. Privacy helps people to leave behind past actions and decisions they may regret as they grow and mature. To encourage personal growth and social integration, it is important that some past misdeeds be shielded from exposure.

Protection of Intimacy, Bodies, and Sexuality

Privacy protects people's bodies, sexuality and gender expression, and intimate relationships from intrusive scrutiny. According to Professor Danielle Citron, protecting privacy helps people "manage the boundaries of their intimate lives" and respects "individuals' choices about whom they entrust with their bodies and intimate information."[10]

Not Having to Explain or Justify Oneself

Privacy matters because people should not always have to justify their thoughts and actions. Many statements and actions that were not intended to be widely disseminated can be misjudged from afar and can lead to embarrassment or worse. Constantly having to worry about how others will perceive such actions is a heavy burden that privacy can help alleviate. The freedom from having to constantly justify oneself is a social value that represents a key difference between a free society and a totalitarian one.

Framing and Metaphors

Technology and privacy are often understood by means of framing and metaphors. *Framing* includes the way that questions are asked, choices are offered, and trade-offs are structured. Frames are involved in the way technology and privacy are described and understood, and particularly in how technology is designed regarding privacy.[1] *Metaphors* are ways of seeing or describing things in terms of something else. Metaphors may elucidate or distort, sometimes doing both simultaneously. As Ryan Calo aptly notes, "Every metaphor is, in its own way, an argument."[2] Metaphors shape the way we think and how we understand technology and privacy.

Framing and metaphors are essential to how we understand and interpret the world. Though the frames and metaphors chosen in a given instance might appear to be true and ineluctable, they are often selected and shaped by humans with particular motivations. They are thus tools of power.

Technology is not a passive player in this game. More than a mere object to be interpreted, technology turns out to be an active participant in its own interpretation, as its design invokes particular framing and metaphors to shape how we understand it.

We must remain constantly aware of framing and metaphors. We can't just rid ourselves of them, as they are too deeply interwoven in our thought, but we can resist allowing any particular frame or metaphor to cast a spell over us. They need to be continuously questioned.

Framing Effects

Framing changes how we perceive things and how we make decisions. One joke I love involves two people from the same religious congregation debating whether they can smoke and pray at the same time. They end the argument at a stalemate. The next week, one of them tells the other that he has the definitive answer from their religious leader. "I asked him, 'Can I smoke when I pray?' and he said 'Absolutely not.'" The other person says that he also spoke to the same leader, who told him the opposite: "I asked: 'Can I pray when I smoke?' and he said 'Of course, you can pray any time you want.'"[3]

Behavioral economist Alessandro Acquisti has conducted many studies to show that the way certain privacy choices are framed can dramatically affect how people decide. For example, many people will not pay extra for privacy, but they are often willing to forgo a benefit in return for privacy—even if the extra cost and the benefit are worth the same amount. Framing the choice of privacy as an added cost versus a trade-off for a benefit thus makes a significant difference in how people choose.[4]

Technological design frames the way that people make decisions about their privacy.[5] Design can involve how choices are presented to people, often through the interface between technology and humans. As a means of mediating the way humans engage with technology, the interface represents both a frame and a metaphor.[6]

Ultimately, the lesson is that the creators of technology have tremendous power because they are designing it. Through interface design, they frame our interaction with it, shaping how we think about it and how we behave. Far too often, the law fails to regulate design, but design is key: Control the design, control the decision.

The Physicality of Machines and Data

New technologies are often depicted by means of metaphors invoking older technologies and practices. Metaphors for digital technologies are often physical: examples of visual metaphors in the digital world include envelopes (for email), locks (for security), trash cans (for deletion), and clouds (for remote data storage). But these metaphors distort how digital technologies work. For example, deleting data is often misunderstood as zapping it out of existence, as if that trash can's contents went straight to a dump incinerator. But "deleted" data actually still exists on a hard drive until it is overwritten.

A struggle is occurring over how AI is to be represented. In science fiction, AI is usually depicted in the form of robots—a physical metaphor. But in reality, the technologies called "AI" today are not robots but algorithms with no physical form. AI algorithms don't think and aren't intelligent. They consist of math plus data. But many people continue to think about AI in anthropomorphic terms—as a digital brain that learns.

It is helpful—almost irresistible—to use metaphors based on things we're familiar with in order to understand what is new and unfamiliar. We can't escape metaphors, but we must be conscious of the ones we use and their distorting effects.

Today, we not only use metaphors that make technologies seem more similar to the physical world than they are, but also metaphors that conceal their physical origins and effects.

Humans in the Machine, Humans in the Data

A revolutionary device invented in 1770 dazzled audiences in Europe for nearly eighty years—the famous Mechanical Turk, a machine that could play chess. The machine consisted of a wooden cabinet with a chessboard on top of it; an automated figure of an Ottoman Turk sitting beside it would take on all comers in games of chess. However, it later turned out that the machine was a fraud—there was actually a human hiding inside.[7]

Although metaphors can anthropomorphize technology, they can also dehumanize it. Our devices are shiny constructions of metal, plastic, and glass, and the data itself appears to exist in some otherworldly realm. But there are always humans behind technology. As Kate Crawford observes, AI involves humans at nearly every point.[8] The data that AI machine-learning algorithms are trained upon is initially created or generated by humans, reflects human discourse, beliefs, and activities, and is often curated by humans. Humans develop the models for algorithms; they are involved in the training process, the evaluation process, and nearly every other step of the way.[9] Although appearing to exist in an ethereal realm, AI can actually be regarded as very physical, as it takes intensive labor by humans—often hard and unpleasant—and it requires a lot of energy and physical resources. AI is, in essence, constructed by flesh, sweat, and toil.

Technology's physical dimensions, especially its human elements, are often concealed—perhaps to delude us into thinking that technology is neutral and objective, free from the taint of human bias. Pulling back the curtain on the Wizard of Oz to reveal a person in the machine diminishes technology's magic—and also its power.

Ultimately, technology is a human capability or tool, an extension of our intelligence. When we talk about technology, we should talk about the humans *in* the machine as well as *before* the machine and *after* the machine.

Metaphors for Understanding Privacy Problems

How should we understand privacy problems caused by digital technologies? It is difficult, if not impossible, to understand technology and privacy outside of framing and metaphors. Even when we think we're avoiding them, we often don't recognize the hidden latticework of frames and metaphors that structures our thoughts. Thus, instead of trying to abandon all framing and metaphors, it is more fruitful to try to change them—to think differently.

Metaphors are also essential for understanding privacy problems. As John Dewey observed, "a problem well put is half-solved." "The way in which the problem is conceived," Dewey elaborated, "decides what specific suggestions are entertained and which are dismissed; what data are selected and which rejected; it is the criterion for relevancy and irrelevancy of hypotheses and conceptual structures."[10]

More than two decades ago, I argued that critics of the increasing collection and use of personal data were often invoking the metaphor of George Orwell's dystopian novel *1984.*[11] In Orwell's chilling world, the government—known as Big Brother—engages in relentless surveillance of citizens. Surveillance cameras are everywhere, particularly in the form of "telescreens"—TV screens in people's homes that watch them back.

I argued then (and still believe) that the Orwell metaphor is incomplete in capturing the problems created when companies (rather than the government) gather and use massive quantities of personal data. Orwell's drab and dreary world involves overt surveillance; the government's goal is to oppress people, to chill the expression of their unique selfhood, and to enforce their conformity to the norm. Posters are tacked up everywhere to remind people that they are being watched. In contrast, today's digital technologies present us with a colorful world that sparkles. Surveillance is hidden, and people don't feel inhibited.

Another metaphor best captures the privacy problems we're experiencing in the Digital Age—the predicament depicted in Franz Kafka's *The Trial.* In the novel, a person is arrested but not told why. A vast bureaucratic court system has assembled a dossier on him and is making decisions about his life, yet he is unable to learn what is going on and is thereby rendered powerless.[12] To his dismay, he discovers that individual control is an illusion; he is at the mercy of an obscure and inscrutable system that exists behind the scenes.

The problems with digital technologies today involve more than the creepiness and chilling effects of being watched. Organizations are using our data on an unprecedented scale to shape what we see, hear, and experience, to influence how we think, and to make decisions about us—all behind the curtain. Even when we're told what's going on, the inner workings of the digital world are too mindbogglingly complex for us to understand.

For example, online social media platforms seem to be free zones where people can share information directly with each other. But they are in fact highly controlled environments, with algorithms working feverishly behind the scenes to shape the conversation. One study of the social media site Twitter (later renamed X) showed that "the algorithm amplifies emotional content, and especially those tweets that express anger and out-group animosity."[13] People are routinely being harassed, threatened, and doxed online, their privacy invaded and their safety compromised.[14] Platform algorithms enhance polarization, leading to a false impression that people's views are more extreme and divisive than they actually are.[15]

We thus must constantly ponder the metaphors we use. While metaphors can open doors to new understandings, they can close other doors. Metaphors can hide from us key dimensions about how digital technologies work and the power wielded over us by those who create and use them. We must be cautious not to let our metaphors become the message.

Myths

Several recurring myths impede the law from addressing problems involving technology and privacy. These myths generally underpin arguments about why the law should take a minimalist approach to regulating technology. But they need to be dispelled, as strong regulation is essential to addressing the challenges technology poses for privacy.

The Myth of the Privacy Paradox

People often say that they cherish privacy but then behave in a seemingly contrary way by failing to protect it and readily relinquishing their personal data. This phenomenon, labeled the "privacy paradox," has become privacy lore; it is constantly discussed and sometimes weaponized to attack privacy regulation.[1] Critics of regulation argue that talk is cheap—that what people *do* is what matters most, and that their behavior shows that they don't actually care much about privacy.

However, the privacy paradox is a myth. It only appears to be a paradox because of conflated issues and flawed logic. The behavior in the privacy paradox involves people making decisions about risk in specific contexts. These contexts often involve particular pieces of personal data disclosed to particular parties with particular expectations of use. In contrast, people's attitudes about privacy are general in nature. Citing individuals' risk decisions in specific contexts to reach broader conclusions about how they value privacy represents a leap in logic. Decisions about risk are different from sentiments about value. Risk involves the potential for harm in a particular situation; value is the overall importance that a person ascribes to something.

The privacy paradox emerges when one tries to measure how much people value privacy by how much they engage in various tasks that I call "privacy self-management," such as reading privacy notices, opting out of certain uses of their data, accessing and correcting their records, requesting that their data be deleted, and other things. But privacy self-management consists of an endless series of chores, and it is ultimately futile. These chores give people something to do and provide the illusion of control. Individuals are blamed when they don't play along in this hollow game, and critics of regulation proclaim that users don't care enough about privacy to justify the law's intervention.

The behavior noted in the privacy-paradox studies doesn't lead to a conclusion that we need less regulation. Instead, it demonstrates that the law must take a significantly different approach: to stop placing the onus on individuals to police their own privacy and take on this burden itself. Instead of trying to put individuals fully in control of their data—which isn't possible—the law should aim to bring the collection, use, and disclosure of personal data under control.

The Myth of Technology Exceptionalism

Far too often, policymakers have urged caution over legal intervention, waiting for a time when things can be better understood and more settled. Policymakers, especially judges and lawmakers, tend to be intimidated by technology and often avoid addressing it because they lack familiarity with it. The law frequently treats new digital technologies as exceptional—that is, distinct enough from everything else that they need to be regulated differently, often with a lighter touch. Far too often, new digital technologies can evade rules that have regulated similar activities involving older analog technologies.[2]

Technology exceptionalism often shields technology from scrutiny and responsibility. Many privacy problems are created by faulty incentives that fail to impose sufficient accountability on technology's creators and users.

The Myth That Regulation Stifles Innovation

Critics of regulation often claim that regulation stifles innovation, bogging down organizations in a morass of paperwork and restrictions, sapping valuable time, and swamping them in costs.

But the notion that innovation and regulation are oppositional is false. Many organizations spend a pittance on privacy-law compliance as a percentage of overall profits. The most effective regulation often involves holding the creators and users of technology accountable for the costs they foist on individuals and society.

The alchemy for innovation isn't anemic regulation; instead, it typically involves bringing together bright, creative people, many of whom want their work to do good. Silicon Valley in California, despite having some of the strongest privacy laws, restrictive business regulation, and high taxes, is where many technology companies are born. These laws haven't driven the innovators away. Innovators are drawn to the Valley because so many other innovators, engineers, and technologists are there – it's where the party is.

Regulation is often a friend of innovation, not a foe. Effective regulation aims to prevent nightmares like Frankenstein's monster, and it can help steer organizations away from innovating in the wrong direction. Regulation might impede those who focus maniacally on building their technologies without concern about what they break. Regulation protects companies that innovate thoughtfully and responsibly by preventing companies that don't from having an unfair advantage.

The Myth That Changes in Degree Don't Matter

Most of the changes ushered in by digital technologies are not radically new. Instead, these changes involve heightening, accelerating, or systematizing things that already are occurring. One common myth is that incremental changes don't warrant dramatic policy changes, and that we should worry mainly about dramatic transformations instead. But as Jack Balkin aptly notes, with new technological developments, we should focus on salience rather than novelty.[3] Technology is about change, and not all change represents a paradigm shift. Many changes caused by technology are incremental, but over time these small movements can be transformative.

Issues of degree matter. Telescopes and eyeglasses may both involve magnification, but they are so different that they aren't equivalent. It is commonly said that a frog dropped into boiling water will leap out but that a frog placed in cool water that is slowly brought to a boil will stay in and get boiled. Like the frog, we fail to act in our own defense as technology slowly accelerates, realizing that we need to do something yet not knowing precisely when or how to act. What makes technological change vexing is that there often is no clear line to be crossed.

Changes in degree can eventually become changes in kind. Speed, size, and fluidity might increase incrementally without a clear break from the past. Many things blend into each other, often with no sharp demarcations between them. But the lack of clear lines shouldn't prevent the law from intervening. Since technology primarily causes changes in degree, the law often has some tools ready for the task. Many technology and privacy problems are, at the core, old problems with new dimensions.

The Myth That the Law Is an Interloper

Skeptics of privacy regulation often see it as meddling with the nature of things. They argue that regulatory intervention interferes with the natural evolution of technology, and thus represents a futile attempt to alter destiny, as in a Sophoclean tragedy.

But the problems involving technology and privacy are not naturally occurring; instead, they are often substantially constructed by the law. Privacy isn't a natural resource that law must protect; instead, it is largely a societal construct developed through law and norms—a set of restraints, protections, physical and mental spaces, freedoms, and rights. Privacy is a form of government intervention as well as freedom from government. It is an architecture of checking and regulating power.

Nor is technology separate from the law. The law not only reacts to technology but also shapes it.[4] The modern data ecosystem—where data is collected, created, and processed—is a product of both law and technology. The data ecosystem is fueled by business and commerce, transactions and contracts—which are all undergirded by an elaborate legal infrastructure. As law professor Amy Kapcynski aptly observes, "companies rely upon law for their power."[5]

Although technology has played a major role in the loss of privacy, the primary culprit is the legal scaffolding of the modern information economy. The law facilitates the collection and transfer of personal data. The law creates incentives that increase the vulnerability of our data. The question is not whether the law should meddle with technology: it already does. The question is which direction the law should proceed in.

The Myth of Technology Neutrality

A common myth is that technology is neutral. Technology is perceived to be detached from human ideology, free from the taint of human bias. Technology is seen as better than humans at making decisions because it doesn't have motivations or emotions and doesn't act irrationally or maliciously.[6]

But this notion is wrong. Technology is designed by humans, so human aims and desires are often baked into it.[7] Technology is deployed by humans, so it can be used in ways that aren't neutral. For instance, surveillance technologies are disproportionately used to target minorities. Many algorithms are trained by data that is polluted with human bias.[8]

While we strive to make technology better than us, we continue to make it in our own image. Like Dr. Frankenstein, we act with hubris when we think our creations can readily transcend our own flaws. For example, I hear countless hopeful statements about how AI will improve upon human decision-making. But we must resist being spellbound by the hype of transcendence. The smudges of human fingerprints are all over technology. As Kate Crawford observes: "Like all technologies before it, artificial intelligence will reflect the values of its creators."[9]

Many algorithms focus on quantifiable data, which creates the illusion of objectivity, neutrality, and truth. Indeed, people often believe that *numbers don't lie*,[10] and numbers are often used to tell a story that seems objective. But quantitative data turns out to be highly manipulable, and it is often strategically curated and presented.[11]

The technology neutrality myth is pernicious because it cloaks bias behind a luminous façade. To effectively regulate technology, we must pull back the curtain and confront its human dimensions.

PART II

DIMENSIONS OF TECHNOLOGICAL CHANGE

How is technology affecting privacy? I'll discuss several ways. This will not be an exhaustive discussion, but an attempt to discuss the changes that are most salient and important.

I have categorized the changes in four general areas: (1) *Information and Knowledge*, where technology affects how information (raw data) is converted to knowledge (processed data); (2) *Judgments and Decisions*, where technology changes how people judge each other and how decisions are made about individuals; (3) *Thought and Behavior*, where technology changes how people think, perceive, and act; and (4) *Power*, where technology changes how power is distributed in society.

Each type of change leads to serious problems for privacy that must be addressed. Briefly, the list is as follows:

Information and Knowledge

Flow. Digital technologies enable personal data to flow more readily than in the nondigital world, making personal data harder to contain and control.

Memory. Digital technologies transform fleeting data into a permanent record.

Obscurity. Finding data is much easier today than ever before, eroding the practical obscurity that undergirds privacy.

Aggregation. Digital technologies enable the combination of small pieces of data into extensive databases over time, revealing much that individuals often don't want to expose.

Inference. Algorithms generate inferences that can reveal facts about people that they didn't expect to be known.

Judgments and Decisions

Prediction. Decisions about people are increasingly being made by algorithmic predictions that ignore people's agency and often are impossible to disprove.

Automation. Automated decisions often fail to account for the nuances of life.

Reputation. Digital technologies make personal reputation more difficult to manage and more precarious.

Consent. Technologies are facilitating the collection and use of personal data without meaningful consent, while often falsely implying that such consent has been obtained.

Thought and Behavior

Expectation. Technology thwarts people's expectations of privacy and erodes those expectations in the process.

Design. The design of technologies manipulates people in profound ways, often leading to choices and behavior about privacy that are contrary to their interests.

Distance. Digital technologies shape the way people perceive distance, often leading to increased sharing of intimate data and to communication that is coarser and more hurtful.

Manipulation. Digital technologies greatly enhance the ability of organizations and fraudsters to manipulate people's behavior and decisions.

Relationships. In personal relationships, technology affects how people share information; in consumer relationships, it enhances the power that companies wield over people.

Power

Control. Through massive data gathering and surveillance, organizations have vast powers to shape people's behavior.

Inequality. The harms of technology disproportionately affect marginalized people.

Identification. Technology enables a more systematic way of identifying people and exercising control over them.

Cost. Technology vastly decreases the cost of processing and spreading data, resulting in the decline of privacy-protective norms and the ability of organizations to amass enormous hoards of data.

Scale. Digital technologies enable the processing of data at an enormous scale, leading to harms affecting countless people.

Harm. Digital technologies create privacy harms that are challenging for the law to address because they are often intangible and dispersed and may be caused by a multitude of different actors.

Vulnerability. The architecture of the modern data ecosystem creates vast vulnerabilities that can be exploited by hackers and fraudsters.

Accountability. Creators and users of technology are often not held accountable for the harms they cause.

* * *

For each technological change affecting privacy, the law often not only fails to address it adequately but also contributes to the problems that arise from it. Many of the problems stem not directly from technology but from prevailing views and myths about technology and privacy. Making headway in privacy protection requires that we think differently.

Information and Knowledge

Flow

It started as a trickle, then became a stream, then a raging river. Modern digital technologies have dramatically increased data flow, the movement of data between people and organizations. And the consequences have been significant. As data circulates more rapidly and extensively, maintaining control of it become much harder. We lose track of who has our data and how it is being used.

A History of Dam Breaks

In the old days, data flow occurred mainly through gossip. But fluttering tongues could only spread data within a limited range, among a group of friends or colleagues, often living nearby each other.

With each new technology, data flow transformed into something faster, broader, and far more indelible. For example, cameras in the late 19th century were large, heavy, and expensive, and photos required people to pose motionless. Kodak's invention of a cheap portable camera revolutionized photography. In 1890 this new technology prompted two young lawyers, Samuel Warren and Louis Brandeis, to write a seminal article, "The Right to Privacy." They worried that these new cameras would enable candid photos without people's consent, which would be dangerous in the hands of the sensationalistic media.[1] Though most newspapers at the time barely used illustrations, let alone photographs, Warren and Brandeis could see the future.

The internet has put the spread of data on steroids. Personal data is now being gathered to an unprecedented degree at an unparalleled pace, is circulating between various organizations in massive quantities, and can be blasted to anywhere in the world in nanoseconds.

Privacy Is About Boundaries, Not Secrecy

The law often treats privacy in a simplistic, binary way: personal data is either secret or exposed. And once data is exposed, the law refuses to provide privacy protections—the cat is out of the bag. I call this notion of privacy the "secrecy paradigm."[2] However, privacy is actually much more complicated. Privacy involves a set of boundaries that modulate the flow of data. Rarely do people keep their data entirely secret; instead, they share it within certain social boundaries—revealing data to friends or family, or to colleagues from work, or to members of affinity groups.

In the law school where I teach, there are different communities of information sharing. The entire school is a community, but within it are subcommunities. In the professor community, we share personal information; we know about each other's lives and families. In the student community, details about students' personal lives circulate in various eddies and streams. But professors won't tell students about the private lives of other professors, and students won't share gossip about other students with professors.

Broader and faster data flow more readily traverses such social boundaries. Before the Digital Age, gossip would often stay locally within a person's social circle, constrained by geography. Now, data can flow almost anywhere in an instant.[3]

Controlling Data Flow

To protect privacy, the law must control data flow. Tracking data flow is essential; otherwise, we won't know who has the data and what is being done with it. Rights, duties, and accountability must flow with the data, and boundaries must be respected.

Regulatory enforcement must also follow the data. Far too often, privacy laws focus only on the entity initially collecting the data and fail to protect the data when it flows to different entities.[4] Large organizations often hire hundreds (sometimes thousands) of companies to process data for them. Direct regulation of these data processors prevents privacy laws from losing their protective powers when data flows from one organization to another.

On social media, people may share personal life details with a curated group of friends. Their privacy settings on the site control who can see the data. But if others breach a boundary and share the information beyond it, sites often do little to protect their users. And when a person shares data with many friends on social media, courts and policymakers often fail to consider it as private. Under the secrecy paradigm, once a secret is out of the bag, then it can't be protected because it isn't deemed to be private.

But privacy isn't about secrecy; it's about maintaining boundaries. The public availability of data doesn't mean that it can't be controlled or protected. Consider how copyright law protects intellectual property. If I write a poem and post it online, it's protected by copyright even though it's publicly viewable. Copyright law is about controlling use; some uses are permitted and some are not. Privacy law should adopt a similar approach.

Privacy is highly contextual.[5] The social boundaries of data flow are nuanced and delicate. The law needs a conception of privacy that understands and enforces these boundaries, not a crude binary conception such as the secrecy paradigm.

Memory

Personal data used to be mostly maintained in people's memories, which are imperfect and fleeting. Eventually everyone who remembers a particular matter will pass on, and the memory of it will flicker out of existence.

Today, data can live on forever. Electronic brains don't forget, though some data does eventually degrade and vanish.[6] Stupid and embarrassing moments are regularly captured and posted online, where they become grist for entertainment.

People remember in fragments and vague impressions; computers remember in exacting detail even the most trivial things that nobody notices. Data about everyday transactions, such as one's purchases and movements, are being captured and stored indefinitely. The burgeoning amount of digital storage makes it easy and cheap to store so much information, and improved search allows data to be retrieved efficiently.

The Virtues of Forgetting

As technology remembers so much more, we are losing the ability to forget.[7] But forgetting is integral to freedom. Embarrassing data can become a permanent scarlet letter, making it difficult or impossible for individuals to grow and move on. Digital memory binds people to the old rattling bones of their past skeletons, and tarnished reputations live on in infamy. However, people are dynamic beings who grow and change throughout life. As John Dewey aptly stated, a person is not "something complete, perfect, finished" but is "something moving, changing, discrete, and above all initiating instead of final."[8] We should afford individuals second chances rather than tethering them to their pasts. The most effective way to do this is to allow information about people's pasts to be forgotten.

Erving Goffman noted that individuals wear different masks and play different roles in life.[9] People present many faces to the world. They have professional roles and personal roles; they are parents, mentors, friends, lovers, partners, employees, and more. These roles bring different expectations and require acting in different ways. These roles also involve different patterns of revealing and concealing information.

The Right to Delete and the Duty of Data Minimization

The law protects against permanent digital memory primarily through two mechanisms: an individual right to delete, and a duty of data minimization.

An individual right to delete, though important, is generally limited in its effect because people don't have the time to make enough deletion requests to wipe clean all the data stored about them. In many cases, people don't even know many of the organizations that possess their data. The right to delete can occasionally be useful, but privacy laws often rely too much on this right. Individuals alone are unable to curtail the burgeoning digital memories about them.[10]

A duty of data minimization, as frequently imposed by privacy laws, is a requirement to retain only the data necessary to achieve the purposes for which it was collected and to delete the data after those purposes have been achieved. In theory, data minimization is a much more powerful way to protect privacy than an individual's right to delete. But there are some practical challenges. Although data minimization is a laudable goal, privacy laws often only articulate it as a rather vague and general principle. To be meaningful, data-minimization must have teeth; there must be auditing to ensure that data is properly purged and enforcement to punish the improper hoarding of data. Otherwise, laws pronouncing a principle of data minimization will be hollow in practice.

Obscurity

Obscurity is a key dimension of privacy.[11] Though we live much of our lives in public places, we tend to assume that nobody is paying attention. But modern surveillance technologies are threatening this obscurity. Conversations can be readily recorded. Movements can be tracked. As people wander around the internet, they sprinkle an extensive amount of personal data along their tracks, which organizations vacuum up into gigantic record systems.

Before the Digital Age, much personal data was shielded through practical obscurity, and finding data from various sources was difficult and time-consuming. But digital technology has upended practical obscurity. Information is now so accessible and searchable that it can be easy to assemble massive dossiers from publicly available sources.

Scraping for AI

The rapid rise of AI has dramatically increased the gathering of personal data online, a practice known as "scraping." Companies today systematically scour the internet for troves of personal data because a massive volume of information is essential to the development of AI. Machine-learning algorithms—the technology that powers many AI systems today—must be trained with data. To make decisions about people or to engage in activity that simulates human behavior, the algorithms must ingest enormous quantities of personal data.

A popular use of AI is for facial recognition technologies. In much of daily life, individuals are mere faces in a crowd, unknown and unidentified. But facial-recognition technology is encroaching on that anonymity by readily identifying people and linking to a dossier about them. With surveillance cameras sprouting up everywhere, people can be tracked wherever they go. Facial recognition systems are trained to recognize people by scraping billions of photos online without people's consent.[12]

Organizations plunder data online to nourish the voracious appetite of their AI beasts. The internet now teems with bots that gobble up data in a feeding frenzy like hogs at the trough. Even though scraping violates longstanding privacy principles in nearly every dimension— ignoring the principle of data minimization and thwarting people's expectations, choices, and consent preferences—such plunder has swiftly become the norm.

Scrapers declare that the data is public and therefore free for the taking. Under the thrall of the secrecy paradigm, many privacy laws allow scraping because they exclude publicly available data from their protection. But the core idea of obscurity is that the public availability of data does not imply the demise of privacy.

The Perils of Public Records

Long before the rise of the internet, open-records laws were passed to enable individuals to shed light on the activities of their government. But today, these laws are being used for a very different purpose – to shed light on the activities of individuals. Many governments today post vast stores of records online with the aim of making them more accessible. And Big Data companies are now gathering personal data from these records—not in order to learn about the workings of the government but to compile dossiers about individuals.

Government law-enforcement agencies are now contracting with Big Data companies to have this information seasoned and spiced with additional data and analysis. Laws originally designed to empower individuals are now twisted into tools to enable the government and large corporations to examine the private lives of individuals. [13]

Beyond the Secrecy Paradigm

Under the archaic secrecy paradigm, the law recognizes as private only things that are completely hidden; once something is exposed to the public—whether by being visible in a public place, publicly available, or part of a public record—then it is no longer private. But in the Digital Age, this binary distinction between private and public is too black-and-white. Between these poles is a crucial gray zone where much of modern life occurs.

In one prescient case from 1989, the US Supreme Court recognized the concept of obscurity. A news-media organization demanded dossiers that the FBI had compiled about citizens under the Freedom of Information Act. Though the Act includes an exemption for privacy, the media organization argued that the data wasn't private because it was already available in various public records that the FBI had scoured to compile the dossiers. In *DOJ v. Reporters Committee*, the Court rejected this argument: "Plainly there is a vast difference between the public records that might be found after a diligent search of courthouse files, county archives, and local police stations throughout the country and a computerized summary located in a single clearinghouse of information."[14] The Court aptly recognized that information scattered in various physical records in different locations takes significant time and resources to find. Though the information isn't secret, its obscurity provides meaningful limits on its accessibility. Gathering personal data and making it readily discoverable makes an enormous difference in the degree of privacy in that data.

In most subsequent cases, however, the Supreme Court has failed to embrace the same reasoning, rejecting a privacy interest in obscurity and instead clinging to the secrecy paradigm. But to effectively protect privacy, the law must break away from this simplistic binary thinking. With a more nuanced understanding of privacy, we can see that making data more widely accessible dramatically affects its privacy.

The government must stop pumping so much personal data into the public domain without restrictions and obligations. Even when users' data is publicly available, platforms must be obligated to protect it. Organizations must be prevented from devouring personal data they find online and using it for whatever purposes they want.

Aggregation

Technology makes it easy to aggregate data. Privacy is often threatened not by a massive violation but instead by the aggregation of many tiny infringements. In what I call "aggregation effect," the merging of small pieces of personal data can reveal much more than the sum of the parts. Aggregation involves gathering data on a large scale and combining disparate pieces of data into digital dossiers about people—akin to assembling a jigsaw puzzle—to form a portrait of them.[15]

Accumulating Data over Time and Harm

Each time we disclose some personal data, it might seem innocuous and unrevealing. As data is aggregated, however, organizations can learn unexpected details about us. To our surprise, our data is combined to reveal facts about our lives that we didn't want to expose.

Privacy harms often are not caused by a single organization at one particular time. Instead, a multitude of organizations do small things that add up little by little. As more pieces of data are collected, used, transferred, and disclosed online, the accumulated circulating data becomes more revelatory.

In some contexts, such as the use of geolocation data, policymakers are awakening to the concept of aggregation. Extensive geolocation tracking of a person's travel will reveal a plethora of details about their lives. The US Supreme Court recognized this fact in *Carpenter v. United States* (2018). Until this case, the Court had long held that anything that could be observed in a public place isn't private. But even though much geolocation data involves movement in public places, in *Carpenter* the Court recognized that geolocation data "provides an intimate window into a person's life."[16] The Court concluded that there is a reasonable expectation of privacy in GPS data, thus providing Fourth Amendment protection and requiring law-enforcement officials to obtain a search warrant to collect it. Many state consumer-privacy laws were passed after *Carpenter*, with nearly all of them deeming geolocation data to be sensitive information subject to stringent protections.

Yet with many other types of personal data, policymakers have failed to recognize the effects of aggregation. As a result, technology is now enabling the aggregation of personal data at an unprecedented rate, and the law is often doing nothing in response.

The Law Must Focus on the Big Picture

The law fails to address the aggregation of personal data because it myopically focuses on each instance of data collection. The law requires organizations to publish a privacy notice to inform individuals about the data being collected about them. Laws diverge about whether to require that people opt in or be given an opportunity to opt out. Either way, users are being asked to make a choice when each piece of data is collected. But because privacy risks rarely can be assessed immediately, this is the wrong moment to decide. And once data is collected, privacy laws often fail to restrict an organization's ability to combine the data and analyze it.

Inference

Inference involves the analysis of personal data to glean new facts about individuals. Modern computing technology has made it much easier to parse large quantities of data to make such inferences.[17]

Unwanted Revelations

Making inferences can invade individuals' privacy by revealing things they want to conceal. In one famous incident reported by the *New York Times*' Charles Duhigg in 2012, the retailer Target created an algorithm to identify pregnant women based on their buying habits. By detecting pregnancy early on, Target calculated that it could entice women to start buying baby products. When the father of a teenage girl began to see many baby ads mailed from the store, he complained that the ads were being sent to the wrong house. But he later found out that his daughter was indeed pregnant.[18]

How was Target's algorithm able to figure out who was pregnant? The algorithm had detected a pattern: Pregnant women frequently buy unscented products, vitamins, and cotton balls.

When the story broke, it became the paradigm example of creepy uses of data analytics. It continues to be discussed to this day, more than a decade later. Sadly, though, the Target executives who created the program didn't learn the right lesson:

> With the pregnancy products, though, we learned that some women react badly. Then we started mixing in all these ads for things we knew pregnant women would never buy, so the baby ads looked random.... And we found out that as long as a pregnant woman thinks she hasn't been spied on, she'll use the coupons. . . . As long as we don't spook her, it works.[19]

Instead of conceding that it is wrong to use data analytics to infer information that people don't willingly reveal, the Target executives concluded that they should just hide what they are doing so people won't become upset.

The Fact and Fiction of Inferences

Inferences are often formed by comparing a person's profile to a large dataset of other profiles and identifying commonalities. The algorithms that produce inferences work best when people are similar to each other, but often perform poorly when there are peculiarities.

There are problems when inferences miss the mark, but also when inferences are spot-on. Error and precision are the edges of a double-edged sword. When wrong, inferences can lead to faulty decisions about people; when right, they can reveal too much about people's private lives.

The Technology-Neutrality Myth

One common myth about data-analysis technology is that it is neutral and free from prejudice. *Data doesn't lie*, the reasoning goes, and *Data-analysis technology doesn't have an ideology or prejudice*. Yet the underlying data often isn't neutral, and it can actually be riddled with prejudice. Data can reflect societal attitudes and behaviors, and these are often tainted with bias.[20] Data is akin to dirty water: whatever is produced with it will be contaminated.

When inferences are used systematically to influence people's decisions and behavior, they actively shape those decisions and behavior toward the patterns revealed in existing data. For example, in 2014 Amazon.com created an AI algorithm to help select which job candidates to hire, hoping that this would make hiring more objective and unbiased. But it had the opposite effect: the algorithm systematically favored males over females. The reason stemmed from the underlying data the AI was trained on: the algorithm was trained to look for applicants similar to those who had been hired in the past, and these people were disproportionately male.[21] By more thoroughly and systematically retaining the bias, the algorithm proved to be far worse than traditional hiring.

Inferences are not merely a reflection of human attitudes and behavior but an active shaper of them. Instead of removing prejudice from data, inferences can reinforce and even increase it.[22] But the myth of neutrality nevertheless persists, which makes the inferences all the more pernicious because they are more trusted.

The Law's Failure to Focus on Inferences

Privacy law often focuses on the collection of data rather than the generation of data through inference.[23] Most privacy laws provide people with the right to correct their data or to consent to the collection of the data, but they often do not allow individuals to address problems in the *inferences* made from their data.

Creating data through inference is the functional equivalent of collecting data. A central protection of many privacy laws is for organizations to limit the collection of personal data to what is necessary for specified purposes. But if organizations can simply generate new data through inferences, then limitations on data collection lose much of their intended effect. The generation of data through inference thwarts people's expectations and turns statements about data collection into lies. The law must consider inferred data as tantamount to collected data.

Judgments and Decisions

Prediction

AI algorithms not only generate inferences about the past and present but also make predictions about the future.[1] The augury of these algorithms involves analyzing vast quantities of data and using probabilities and statistics to calculate what the future holds in store. Increasingly, algorithmic predictions are being made about human behavior: Will a person commit a crime in the future? Will a person pay back a loan? Will a person be a successful employee? Will a person be a good student?

Decisions based on predictions affect people's opportunities and freedom. Individuals can be denied employment based on predictions about their health. They can be singled out for extra scrutiny at the airport based on predictions that they might engage in terrorism. They can be targeted for law-enforcement investigations based on predictions that they might commit a crime.[2]

Repudiation of Agency

Algorithmic predictions pose a significant threat to individual self-determination. Such predictions not only forecast the future but also can shape and control it.[3] They diminish people's ability to be the authors of their own destiny.

To condemn people before they act is a repudiation of their agency. The 2022 science-fiction movie *Minority Report* depicts a harrowing dystopia where the police devise a system to predict future crime and convict people before they have done anything. Punishing people before they act denies them their ability to be the authors of their own lives. As Professor Carissa Véliz contends, "by making forecasts about human behavior just like we make forecasts about the weather, we are treating people like things. Part of what it means to treat a person with respect is to acknowledge their agency and ability to change themselves and their circumstances."[4]

Self-Fulfilling Prophecies

Algorithmic predictions enable organizations to better manipulate and control human behavior. In the words of physicist Dennis Gabor, "the best way to predict the future is to create it."[5] Predictions can become self-fulfilling prophecies, as they can lead to interventions that reinforce the predicted outcome.[6] For example, a prediction that people fitting a certain profile are likely to be criminals could lead to more arrests and convictions of these individuals—not because the profile is true but because the police are focusing on those fitting the profile. Although this extra focus might result in catching more culprits, this could mean not that those profiled are more likely to be engaged in criminal activity but rather that some criminal activity is likely to be revealed when many people are subjected to police investigation.

Algorithmic predictions don't work like a crystal ball, magically presenting a vision of the future. Instead, such predictions are probabilities generated from historical data, and what they present is really a picture of the past, not the future. The assumption behind these predictions is that yesterday's behavioral patterns will be the same tomorrow. But this isn't always the case: in many circumstances, data from the past is skewed by bias, discrimination, inequality, and privilege. Thus, algorithmic predictions often perpetuate inequality and bias, projecting it into the future.[7]

Data Is Human and Not Everything Is Expected

Algorithmic predictions are extolled as superior to human predictions—free from bias and other human taints.[8] But such claims are questionable. Under the myth of technology neutrality, data is assumed to be objective, but data is no better than the society that produces it. Data is human: It is generated by humans, collected by humans, curated by humans, and used by humans, and it frequently reflects their particular prejudices and ideologies.[9]

Algorithms depend upon such data to make predictions. These predictions may look trustworthy, but they are tainted if they are baked with contaminated ingredients.

Algorithmic predictions typically ignore people's unique attributes and life stories.[10] Even if a person is on a path toward behaving as an algorithm predicts, there's always the possibility that he or she may swerve from that path. Decisions based on algorithmic predictions exalt statistical regularities, but history has often swiveled on the unexpected. Prior to discovering Australia, Europeans had thought that all swans were white; when they arrived in Australia, they were astonished to see black swans. Nassim Nicholas Taleb uses this anecdote to issue a general warning—that we should be humble with our predictions. According to Taleb, we "may be good at predicting the ordinary, but not the irregular."[11]

Lack of Due Process

Decisions based on predictions violate the fundamental tenet of justice that people shouldn't be penalized for things they haven't done. [12] When the justice system relies on predictions, it judges and condemns people based on things they didn't do and might never do.

Many privacy laws provide a right to rectify incorrect data—but this right is useless where predictions are concerned.[13] Because they involve occurrences that haven't yet happened, predictions can't be assessed as accurate or inaccurate. Most algorithmic predictions exist in a twilight between truth and falsity: they are not yet true, nor are they false. For example, how could you disprove a prediction that you will commit a terrorist act at some point in the future? The accuracy of such a prediction can only be determined after you die.

In the legal case *Wisconsin v. Loomis*, a judge sentenced a defendant by using an algorithmic system called the Correctional Offender Management Profiling for Alternative Sanctions (COMPAS) which predicted that the defendant was a high risk for recidivism. Based on this prediction, the judge meted out a long sentence.[14] The defendant contended that his sentence violated due process because the algorithm generated its predictions from the data of others, and thus he was punished on the basis of what other people did. The Wisconsin Supreme Court rejected his argument, observing that the judge wasn't required to accept the algorithm's prediction. But the judge did in fact accept it, and studies show that people often defer to algorithmic output.[15]

Even more troubling was the fact that the defendant was denied information about how the algorithm worked, because the company that created it claimed such information was a trade secret.[16] Though the company insisted its algorithm was fair and unbiased, a later study would demonstrate that COMPAS actually disfavored black defendants.[17]

Automation

With new technologies, automation has moved from the manufacturing assembly line to the making of decisions about people. Because of its efficiency, automated decision-making is being used on an ever-increasing scale.

Automated decision-making is touted as more objective and neutral than human decision-making, which is plagued by slowness, constrained by limited information, clouded by emotion, and soiled with bias. Human judgment is awful, the argument goes, and machines are superior. But this argument is flawed, for it makes a faulty comparison, as if machines just think like humans without the shortcomings. Humans and machines decide in fundamentally different ways; automated decisions lack key dimensions of human decisions; and machines frequently hide but don't eliminate human biases.[18]

Quantifiable vs. Qualitative Data

Automation attempts to mimic human judgment to some degree, but often falters in capturing the nuance and nimbleness of the human mind. To a considerable extent, automated judgments rely on standardization, and this can lead to mechanical decisions that are less tailored to the multifarious contexts and complexities of human life. Automated judgments simplify, reducing things to patterns and commonalities.[19]

Although vast quantified datasets can help us see certain overall trends and regularities, they typically smooth over differences and peculiarities. Consider the exuberant observation by Lambert Adolphe Jacques Quetelet, a pioneer of statistics in the early 19th century: "The greater the number of individuals observed, the more do individual particularities, whether physical or moral, become effaced, and leave in a prominent point of view the general facts, by virtue of which society exists and is preserved."[20] But individual divergences are valuable and insightful; they enlarge and deepen our understanding of the complexities of human behavior. They shouldn't be sanded away.

Data that is not readily quantifiable can often be ignored by automated systems. Automation involves translating the rich tapestry of life into simpler patterns. The engines of automation run on refined data, filtering out idiosyncratic details that are hard to quantify.[21] These details are frequently important, however; indeed, they form the rich texture of life. Critiquing what he calls the "tyranny of metrics," Jerry Muller aptly invokes the famous saying "Not everything that can be counted counts, and not everything that counts can be counted."[22]

W. H. Auden's poem "The Unknown Citizen" depicts the shallowness of statistical facts about individuals. The poem describes fragments of data about a man's life compiled by the Bureau of Statistics: he was married, had five children, worked in a factory, owned common items, and so on. The poem ends:

Was he free? Was he happy? The question is absurd:
Had anything been wrong, we should certainly have heard.[23]

The narrator can't perceive the superficiality of the objective data and how it fails to capture the most important aspects of the man's life.

The Law's Shortcomings

The law struggles in dealing with automated decisions. The EU's General Data Protection Regulation (GDPR) and a few other laws do provide special protections against "solely" automated decisions.[24] But many automated decisions are only partially automated, so these special protections don't apply.

More generally, many laws seek to address automated decisions by requiring transparency regarding the programming involved.

However, transparency is often not meaningful in such cases, since the algorithms used to make automated decisions can be far more sophisticated than most people can understand. Even learning about the logic of automated decisions may not be enough, because the automated decisions depend upon the personal data of millions of people, which can't be shared with individuals without violating everyone's privacy. Without knowing the data that algorithms are trained on, it can be difficult or impossible to evaluate certain automated decisions.

Ultimately, the law must delve into the substance of automated decisions. But thus far, it has only nibbled around the edges without going to the core.

Humans in the Loop

One of the GDPR's special protections against *solely* automated decisions is to allow people to demand human involvement. But merely adding a human into the loop can't cure the ills of automation, since humans often perform quite poorly when evaluating automated decisions. Unfortunately, the GDPR doesn't provide guidance about how humans should review automated decisions.[25]

As professor Ben Green aptly notes, human and machine decision-making are so different that combining them can be like trying to mix oil and water. Algorithmic decision-making is used for its consistency and strict adherence to rules, whereas human decision-making involves "flexibility and discretion." When policymakers call for humans to oversee algorithms, they ignore this "inherent tension."[26]

Automation typically achieves efficiency, but at the cost of producing simplistic and distorted outcomes that omit the full flavor of life. The problem isn't technology itself but rather how humans think about technology, and specifically any presumptions that automation is better than human decision-making and is neutral. These presumptions are false; human and machine decisions are fundamentally different, and each has virtues and vices. Automated decisions are far from neutral. The law, unfortunately, focuses mostly on the process of how automated decisions are made, but addressing process alone can't solve all the problems arising from automation. Ultimately, the law's goal should be to ensure that decisions are sound, whether they are made by machines or humans. And all decisions, even automated ones, depend on good human judgment.

Reputation

Reputation is essential for social relations, employment, and friendship. A person's reputation depends upon the opinions of others, which are often formed by fragments of information patched together from gossip, experiences, and a multitude of other sources. Each of us exists in many different versions—that is, as varying interpretations in the minds of those who know us or know about us. Our lack of agency over these interpretations is one of the most precarious aspects of life.

In the past, when people lived in small villages, everyone knew about each other. There were few strangers, and even when one didn't know someone, one could ask around and find out the person's reputation. But urbanization, a ballooning population, and greater mobility have wiped away the social familiarity of yesteryear. Most of us now live in a world of unknown faces. And digital searches have replaced the reputations formerly earned in smaller communities. These new digital reputations pose troubling new issues.[27]

Online Data Fragments and Gossip

Before the internet and social media, people's spheres of knowledge were constrained; an individual could only become acquainted with a limited number of other individuals. Today, with the internet, a person can contact people round the world.

The internet is, among other things, a miasma of gossip. Data fragments online can often paint a superficial portrait of a person. Online data is dubious and unfiltered, and it gushes from countless sources without much thought about the consequences.

Unfortunately, ugly data is often stickier than pleasant data. The stain of salacious data can't readily be scrubbed; instead, it tends to settle deep in the fibers of the mind. Today a tainted online reputation can singe and even burn its owner. For many people, the scars of a wounded reputation can be life-altering injuries, and trolling, doxing, and cyberbullying are causing an endless series of tragedies, from breakdowns to suicides.[28]

When it comes to defamation, technology provides liars with sophisticated tools: fake voices, fake images, fake profiles, and fake videos.[29] Anything can be spoofed, from an email address to a phone number. In today's age of disinformation, the hope that truth will win out in the marketplace of ideas is quaint. Instead, we should recall an oft-quoted line attributed to Mark Twain: "A lie can travel halfway around the world before the truth puts on its shoes." Ironically, the history of this quote proves its point: its attribution to Twain is actually false.[30]

When people turn to the law to protect themselves from gossip or smears, courts often force them to expose their own names in lawsuits to vindicate their reputation. Though it is within a court's discretion to allow people to sue under a pseudonym, most courts are unwilling to do so.[31] The result is perverse: to obtain legal protection, people must increase the exposure of the very information that has tarnished their reputations.

Protection from the Knives of Human Judgment

Reputation is increasingly hard to escape. In the past, a person could move to a new place and start anew. Now, people are prisoners of their past; data follows them wherever they go. Gossip is no longer fleeting; it can exist forever.[32]

But gossip rarely leads to truth. Instead, it represents fragments of information about a person, which can be tossed out mercilessly like scraps of meat to a pack of wolves. Though it is quite difficult, if not impossible, to fully know an individual, people often rush to judgment based on incomplete information.[33] Human judgment can be unfair, biased, hypocritical, and often searing. People rarely take the time to learn about the whole person they are judging, so the individual remains a puzzle with most of the pieces missing.

We don't have a strong command over our reputations. The best way to control our reputation is to curate the information that others know about us. Control over the circulation of our personal data can give us a small degree of protection, fragile yet essential. When we lose this ability, we become helpless.

Unfortunately, the law in the United States facilitates the spread of reputation-harming data. Section 230 of the Communications Decency Act (1996) immunizes platforms from being held responsible for malicious information, even when they are aware that the information is defamatory or invasive of privacy, and even when the platforms encourage and facilitate such content.[34] The result is an explosion of damaging gossip online that people are helpless to stop.

The Scored Society: Mechanized Reputation

At the corporate level, technology has enabled mechanized methods of assessing people's reputations. The credit reporting system in the United States is dominated by three mammoth companies, which feast relentlessly on personal data. The data in individuals' dossiers is crunched through an algorithm to give people credit scores that are used for licensing and employment decisions, as well as to determine whether they qualify for loans and what interest rates they are offered.

There is scant due process in these modern reputation systems. The entities that design the scoring systems wield tremendous power and control.[35] They decide who has been naughty or nice, and they do so in ways that promote the behavior they desire.

Another problem with many reputation systems is that they are reductive and flawed. They reduce reputation to a formula based on quantifiable metrics, ignoring complex qualitative information. The simplistic scores they produce appear to be objective and meaningful but are relied on primarily because they are cheap and convenient.

Reputation systems are not just creatures of technology; they are constructed in part by the law. For example, the Fair Credit Report Act (FCRA) facilitates the credit-reporting system, bathing the credit-reporting companies in immunities from many types of lawsuits. Although the law provides some controls on credit reporting, these controls are far from adequate.

Consent

New technologies poses significant challenges to people's ability to consent to the collection, use, and disclosure of their personal data. Under most privacy laws, consent makes permissible a wide array of data collection and processing. Websites, devices, and software continually attempt to induce people to consent (or pretend that people have consented) to data practices that are risky, troublesome, and unexpected.

To be meaningful, consent must not be unduly manipulated or coerced. And consent must be informed: people must be able to weigh the costs and benefits of consenting. Unfortunately, most privacy consent falls far short of these goals. In fact, privacy consent could almost be called a complete fiction.[36]

False Legitimacy

Philosopher Heidi Hurd refers to consent as a form of "moral magic," instantly transforming something that would otherwise be illegal or immoral into something that is permissible. Consent, she aptly notes, "turns a trespass into a dinner party; a battery into a handshake; a theft into a gift; an invasion of privacy into an intimate moment; a commercial appropriation of name and likeness into a biography."[37] Consent provides legitimacy—the law's equivalent of a blessing—and legitimacy bestows power.

In the realm of privacy, the law today allows dubious or even nonexistent consent to pass as valid, conferring unwarranted legitimacy on data collection, use, and disclosure.[38] Thus, consent in privacy ends up as a form of dark magic, a malevolent sorcery that falsely legitimizes troublesome and unwanted data practices and wrongly bequeaths power to organizations to do whatever they want with people's data.

The Mirage of Meaningful Consent

Obtaining consent in privacy law generally involves one of two approaches: (1) the *notice-and-choice* approach, or (2) the *express-consent* approach. Neither succeeds in working effectively.

The notice-and-choice approach is employed for most data collection in the United States. Organizations post a privacy notice with information about how they collect, use, and disclose personal data. Individuals are often given a choice to opt out; if that is not an option, they can stop doing business with the organization. But since many privacy laws hold that inaction implies consent, those who don't opt out are assumed to have consented.

The notice-and-choice approach is a charade.[39] Hardly anyone reads privacy notices,[40] and inaction can't plausibly be considered consent. The law attempts to turn nothing into something, bestowing upon organizations a fictitious "consent" that gives them the license to use data as they desire. But this ruse is little better than the hocus-pocus of a trickster.

Under the EU's GDPR, in contrast, consent must be express—an affirmative indication of agreement, such as clicking a button or checking a box.[41] But even this more rigorous form of consent can verge on the illusory. People are often prodded to consent at times when they are least interested in thinking about the decision. The benefits of technologies are often instantaneous, and people receive immediate gratification for consenting. Individuals' privacy concerns, by contrast, are often vague and abstract, with uncertain consequences far in the future. Unsurprisingly, people almost always consent—but the choice is rigged.

Lack of Understanding

Many people can't understand the consequences of consenting to the collection, use, or disclosure of their data. The real risks can't be discerned unless people know what will happen in the future, when their data will often be combined with other data, analyzed by algorithms, and used to make inferences, predictions, and decisions. Many algorithms—especially AI algorithms—are far too complicated for the ordinary person to understand.

The Problem of Scale

Even if people could somehow learn enough to meaningfully consent to one particular instance of the collection and use of their data, there are thousands of organizations collecting and using their data, many of which are engaging in a multitude of activities, each one requiring consent. We lack the time to read so many privacy notices or to learn enough to make informed decisions. In today's digital age, there is so much data collection, use, and disclosure that obtaining consent each time is simply impractical.[42]

The Law's Futile Attempt to Fix Consent

Though privacy laws have endeavored to fix the consent process by making notices more conspicuous, users still don't read them.[43] Though many laws mandate that notices be easy to understand, simplistic privacy notices can't accurately describe the implications of consenting to the collection, use, and disclosure of personal data. Vapid statements such as "We care about your privacy" and "We protect your data with reasonable security measures" are meaningless. Privacy is complicated—even for experts. I've studied privacy for a quarter century and I still don't know enough to make thoughtful privacy choices. To properly evaluate the risks of providing data to an organization, I would need to talk with its chief privacy officer and discuss the various technologies with the engineers. I would need to review all privacy impact assessments, algorithms, the data the algorithms are trained on, the data-transfer agreements, data-security measures, and so on. And I'd have to do this for thousands of organizations.

In most situations involving technology and personal data, consent can never truly be meaningful, and the law is making things worse by pretending that it can. Instead, the law should accept that, in almost all cases, privacy consent is unavoidably fictional.

Murky Consent

The law often treats consent as a simple binary: either people consent—granting a license to use their personal data—or they don't consent. It's all or nothing. But consent should instead be understood as a continuum between full consent and non-consent.[44] Most situations involving privacy fall somewhere in the middle of the spectrum and involve an ambiguous, contingent, and troubled consent, which I refer to as "murky consent."[45]

Murky consent should not confer the same legitimacy as full consent. Instead of granting nearly complete power to gather and use data, murky consent should provide a limited and highly restricted license.

Rather than try to turn the fictions of consent into facts, the law should lean into the fictions and embrace the fact that most privacy consent is murky. Murky consent lacks the legitimacy of full consent, and the law should reduce the power such consent confers. When murky consent is involved, the law should impose certain rigorous duties: (1) a duty to obtain consent appropriately, (2) a duty to avoid thwarting reasonable expectations, (3) a duty of loyalty, and (4) a duty to avoid unreasonable risk.

The duty to obtain consent appropriately would add a small degree of integrity to the fiction; although even good-faith efforts to obtain consent are likely to fail, the law shouldn't allow duplicity and manipulation. The duty to avoid thwarting reasonable expectations would aim to ensure that people will not be surprised when they learn about how their data is being used. The duty of loyalty would require that organizations place the interests of consenting individuals first—that is, ahead of their own interests. Finally, the duty to avoid unreasonable risk would guarantee that people aren't consenting to practices that are a bad risk for them. By ensuring that people can't consent to things that are beyond their reasonable expectations, not in their interest, or unreasonably risky, these duties would act as a backstop to consent.

Having obtained consent, an organization today can do nearly anything it wants with a person's data, no matter how bad the consequences might be for that person. The approach of murky consent, in contrast, essentially entails that *if the story of individual consent is fictional, then the law should guarantee that it ends happily ever after for individuals.*

Thought and Behavior

Expectation

Technology regularly thwarts people's expectations. Users are increasingly discovering to their chagrin that their personal data is being collected, used, and disclosed in ways they never expected and often far more extensively and problematically. But as expectations of privacy are increasingly thwarted, the law has responded weakly, with a shrug or sometimes not at all.

Thwarted Consumer Expectations

The law often trivializes thwarted expectations of privacy. Many courts don't view broken promises about privacy as harmful, and they typically deny plaintiffs a remedy. In one case, in which a bank sold personal data to third parties in violation of its privacy notice, the court dismissed the case for a lack of harm because people "were merely offered products and services which they were free to decline."[1] Essentially, the court let the bank get away with lying.

Because most people don't read privacy notices, their expectations are largely based on mistaken preexisting notions. A majority of people falsely believe that when a website has a privacy policy, it won't share personal data with other companies.[2] Little is done to correct these faulty assumptions, even though they may play a major role in users' decisions. The law typically fails to force organizations to make any attempt to correct such mistaken views.[3]

Expectations are also frequently thwarted when users make errors in their privacy settings on social-media sites. In one study, 100 percent of people made an error in their social-media privacy settings: "every participant was sharing something they wished to hide or was hiding something they wished to share."[4] Far too often, people's expectations are not aligned with how their data is collected, used, and disclosed.

Expectation Is the Wrong Focus for Government Surveillance

For government surveillance, the law has long focused on reasonable expectations of privacy. In the view of the courts, the Fourth Amendment to the US Constitution provides protections against government information gathering and surveillance only when people have a reasonable expectation of privacy.[5]

The reasonable-expectation-of-privacy test turns on how judges conceive of privacy, which has been notoriously difficult to conceptualize, with many attempts being far too narrow. In its Fourth Amendment cases, the US Supreme Court has conceived of privacy in crabbed ways that have diminished Fourth Amendment protection. Since many of these cases were decided long before the digital revolution of the 21st century, the Court didn't realize the full implications of its decisions. For example, in the 1970s the Court established the *third-party doctrine*, which holds that there is no reasonable expectation of privacy in data maintained by third parties.[6] But with modern digital technologies, third parties often possess an extensive amount of people's personal data: records of purchases, internet browsing, finances, communications, and more. In the old analog world, the government would need to search one's home to learn about what one was reading, writing, or doing. But today, all this data is in the hands of third parties: merchants, websites, internet service providers, platforms, cloud service providers, and others.

The Court has also held that people lack a reasonable expectation of privacy in anything they discard.[7] But our trash is a grimy compendium of our lives: products consumed, medication bottles, writings, notes, and countless other items revealing intimate information. Following the Supreme Court's logic, lower courts have held that the government can, among other things, follow people around and scoop up discarded food or other items to analyze DNA.[8]

Additionally, the Supreme Court has held that the government can use sense enhancement technology without violating a reasonable expectation of privacy. For example, government agents can fly above people's property to monitor or investigate them and even use a high-tech camera with powerful magnification to take photos.[9]

The "reasonable expectation of privacy" test is flawed not only because of a myopic conception of privacy but because it wrongly focuses on expectations.[10] Privacy expectations diminish as technology advances. As people become accustomed to living in a world of ubiquitous data collection, constant surveillance, and comprehensive tracking, they expect fewer things to be private and receive less protection as a result. Receding legal protection further erodes privacy expectations, resulting in a downward spiral to hardly any protection at all.[11]

The law should focus on the privacy that society *desires*, not the privacy that society *expects*. Privacy laws and protections are most often created not because people expect privacy but because they want to combat a threat to privacy.[12] Privacy protections are most needed when privacy is desired but isn't expected.

Design

Increasingly, technological design is exercising profound control over individuals. As Joel Reidenberg observed, the law isn't the only source of rules; technological design also generates rules, and can in fact even be more powerful than the law.[13] The design of software, websites, and electronic devices controls what people can and can't do, how people behave, how people interact with others, the way people make decisions, how much personal data they disclose, and many other things. Though policymakers have been reluctant to regulate design, it's nearly impossible to regulate technology without addressing design.

Design, Perception, and Behavior

Through design, technologies can affect our perception and distort our sense of reality. Surveillance and tracking devices are becoming increasingly smaller and more inconspicuous. Thus, we often can't see if we're being recorded, and we don't know if our data is being analyzed or how.

A key way in which design affects attitudes and behavior is through the interface between users and their devices, software, websites, or apps. Interfaces are designed to shape user experiences by controlling the look and feel of technology. In an insightful book about interfaces, journalist Steven Johnson observes that the world of computers is so alien to users that it requires an interface to translate it into comprehensible form: "Our only access to this parallel universe of zeros and ones runs through the conduit of the computer interface, which means that the most dynamic and innovative region of the modern world reveals itself to us only through the anonymous middlemen of interface design."[14]

The way we experience the internet is shaped by design choices. We don't have direct access to the internet; our access is instead mediated by design, which directs what we see. Designers control the default settings on websites, which can be initially set to maximize data collection, sharing, and use. Designers shape how readily people can opt into or out of certain data uses. Designers code the algorithms that determine the content we see on platforms. The more we share and engage, the more tech companies benefit financially. So, unsurprisingly, the interfaces often nudge, cajole, and manipulate us to share and engage.

Design Isn't Neutral

Technology and tech design are widely viewed today as value-neutral. But as legal scholar Woodrow Hartzog aptly states in his groundbreaking book *Privacy's Blueprint*, "Design is never neutral. It is political."[15] Many design choices about privacy are deliberately made based on particular aims and trade-offs. These are moral policy decisions.

The privacy implications of design choices typically receive insufficient attention today, and this is a moral failing. For example, the attempt by many online platforms to maximize user engagement often comes at the cost of polarization, harassment, cyberbullying, and other harms. Encouraging users to share personal data can lead to their oversharing or disclosing intimate secrets, which they might later regret.

Design Depends upon a Conception of Privacy

In what is often referred to as "Privacy by Design," several laws require that organizations design products, services, and practices with privacy in mind.[16] Unfortunately, these legal provisions often leave it to the individual organizations to design for privacy without providing much guidance.

Privacy by Design is only as good as the underlying conception of privacy. If the conception is poor or incomplete, the design will be bad. In many instances, the conception of privacy is not explicitly stated, often because very little thought was ever given to it. But there is at least an implicit conception of privacy at play in these instances, and it affects what is and isn't protected.

"We're building privacy into the architecture," various organizations often say when designing technology. Sometimes they'll use a cooking analogy: "We're baking privacy in." But what is the "privacy" that is being designed or baked? Without a proper conception of privacy, Privacy by Design is like constructing a building without a blueprint or baking a cake without a recipe.

In many cases, the "privacy" being baked in is missing several key ingredients. In his interviews with tech engineers, law professor Ari Waldman found that most engineers thought of privacy as merely involving notice and data security.[17] But true privacy involves so much more, including providing meaningful controls on data, specifying how long data should be retained, minimizing the use of data to what is necessary, mitigating any risks of harm, and avoiding unexpected uses of data. Privacy by Design should be founded on a thorough consideration of what privacy is and how it is implicated in design choices. Privacy by Design should be approached with an appreciation for its profound importance, its moral dimensions, and its significant difficulty.

The Law's Timidity

As Woodrow Hartzog convincingly demonstrates, the law can't adequately regulate privacy without regulating design, as privacy is inextricably entwined in the architecture of technology.[18] Unfortunately, the law only regulates design in a timid way. Because of fears of second-guessing technologists, most laws shy away from regulating design, and those that do regulate design are often quite vague and do little beyond stating that privacy should be considered in the design process. Without meaningful standards, review, or accountability, Privacy by Design requirements are hollow.

The fact is, the law can regulate design without micromanaging technologists. For example, the law could demand that any surveillance device indicate to people that it is recording, whether by making devices light up when recording or by using other obvious signals (that much could be left up to the designers).

Only a few laws, such as the GDPR, mandate default settings to maximize privacy. Since many people don't change their default settings, which are often set to maximize information sharing or exposure, they are unwittingly sharing more data than they realize. More laws should follow the lead of the GDPR and require privacy-protective default settings.

Overall, the law must become bolder and not shrink from the challenge of regulating design. And when the law regulates design, it must have meaningful goals and not rely on companies to adopt their own conceptions of privacy, which are often thin and incomplete.

Distance

Technology alters our perceptual and emotional distance from the things that it mediates. Altering distance affects how we perceive and understand things and how we behave and interact with others.

Perceptual and Emotional Distance

In the non-digital world, we make decisions from a particular vantage point and from a physical body. We have a location and context, and hence a certain distance from the things we judge and interact with—a distance that is both perceptual and emotional.

With perceptual distance, when far away we don't see unique details that would be visible in close proximity. Emotional distance involves the extent of our emotional investment in a particular matter. Consider José Ortega y Gasset's analogy to a scene in which a man is dying and four people are at his bedside: his wife, a doctor, a journalist, and a painter. Each observes the death from a different emotional distance. The wife is naturally the closest. For the doctor, the dying man is a professional matter. The journalist views the death as an occasion for a news story. The painter is the most distant, focusing only on the man's appearance and perhaps even finding beauty in the event. Ortega concludes that the contrast in emotional distance between the wife and the painter leads them to witness the death so differently that they might as well be observing different events.[19]

Technology dramatically alters emotional distance. On social media, people often communicate with each other in a more emotionally distant way than in person. Lacking a visual reaction to what they say, their distance makes them feel less accountable and makes other people seem less real, less human.

Distance, Data Sharing, and Design

Distance also affects how people share online. People often share online from the solitude of their own rooms. Without a physically present audience, they are inclined to be less inhibited about revealing intimate details about their lives to thousands of people, whereas if they were on a stage with thousands of faces staring back at them, many of the same people would barely utter a word.

Digital technologies often are intentionally designed to produce a particular perceptual and emotional distance. A social-media interface, for example, could attempt to visually simulate the size of a person's audience or use other means to reduce distance. But social-media companies want to avoid giving people stage fright; in order to encourage data sharing, they don't want people to restrain themselves.

Distance and Decision-Making

Digital technologies also facilitate decision-making based on statistical data, which is a more distant way of deciding. As law and economics professor Guido Calabresi observes, we value real lives more than statistical lives. We respond emotionally to the plight of actual people, which is why we are willing to support expensive rescues. But when lives are reduced to numbers rather than faces or stories, such statistical lives are often readily sacrificed in ways that real lives are not.

Technology often increases the distance between decisions and their effects. Click on a button, and something terrible might happen to people, but clicking is effortless, and the tragic consequences are not immediately witnessed.[20] People often do and say things online that they would never do in person because they don't see the consequences of their hurtful actions and words.

Technology also facilitates making decisions about people en masse. This can be highly efficient. Consider credit scoring, a highly automated way of making loan decisions. Unlike actually meeting with individuals and getting to know them, credit scoring involves using a formula based on quantifiable data to reduce each person to a credit score. Because learning about individuals is time-consuming, credit scoring is obviously an efficient way to make decisions, but it inevitably omits key details about people and their lives.

Decisions made from a distance aren't necessarily bad, but because of the distance, such decisions fail to consider the nuances, idiosyncrasies, and human elements of a situation. The law should address the effects of distance, as it plays a profound role in the way people behave and decide.

Manipulation

The increased power to gather and use personal data enables organizations to more effectively manipulate people. Manipulation involves exercising undue influence on people's decisions and behavior, threatening their autonomy and turning them into puppets with invisible strings.[21] Manipulation can work in a cycle: users are manipulated into sharing personal data, which can then be used to further manipulate them.

Puppet Masters

Studies by Daniel Kahneman, Amos Tversky, and others have revealed systematic biases and heuristics in the way that people make decisions,[22] and the ways that changes in language, framing, and context can dramatically alter human decisions.

In the past, hucksters manipulated on a small scale through cunning, and their tricks were often detectable. But with technology, manipulation is now carried out by code. Manipulation today is architected into designs and interfaces, and it is far more clandestine than the wiles of snake-oil peddlers.

Technology amplifies manipulation, turning it from an art into a science and deploying it on a grand scale. With more personal data, manipulators can learn how particular people make decisions, giving them a window into the mechanics of their minds. By analyzing the data, algorithms identify the most effective ways to induce desired behaviors.

Dark Patterns

The law has long addressed manipulation by punishing fraud and deception. But when manipulation is architected into technological design, the law often skitters away, disinclined to second-guess technologists.

In an interesting and hopeful development, the reframing of manipulative designs as "dark patterns" has sparked bolder legal responses. The term "dark pattern," coined by Harry Brignull in 2010, refers to a structural dimension of websites, apps, and technologies that tricks people into making decisions against their self-interest.[23] Some dark patterns put users through tedious ordeals to impede them from selecting privacy-protective options. Other dark patterns, known as "roach motels," make it easy to agree to share data but difficult to stop. By hiding privacy choices in obscure places, developers force users to engage in a scavenger hunt to find them.

The use of the sinister term "dark pattern" has emboldened lawmakers to regulate, and privacy laws are starting to address these manipulative designs.[24] Lawmakers find it far more palatable to confront "dark patterns" than to restrict programs neutrally labeled as "technological designs," which could be viewed as stifling innovation and second-guessing engineers.

The term "dark pattern" represents a brilliant shift in metaphor, demonstrating how changing the framing of a technological issue can dramatically affect the direction and effectiveness of the law.

Relationships

We live in a web of relationships with others, which play profound roles in our lives. But technology can alter the power dynamics of a relationship. When one party to a relationship has a dossier of information about the other party, the party with the information often has greater power to control or manipulate the other party. Technology also can interfere with valuable relationships by undermining the confidentiality upon which they depend.

Trust and Intimacy

People form relationships of trust with others, and will share more information about themselves as that trust grows. Technology can induce people to trust individuals or organizations when such trust is not yet warranted. In many cases, it might be safer and more prudent not to confer trust so readily.

Technology can unduly foster trust by enabling dangerous people to disguise themselves so that the sheep can't spot the wolves amongst them. Predators can readily befriend children online, and fraudsters can readily spoof friends, colleagues, and organizations. Technology makes it easy to mimic how things look or sound. AI can be used to clone people's voices or to generate fake images or videos. Our eyes and ears become less able to detect when something is off.

In the new gig economy, technologies are encouraging people to place more trust in strangers. For example, people who are reluctant to hitchhike might readily use a ride-sharing app, which clothes the situation in the vestments of professionalism and trustworthiness, and hop into the car of a stranger even when the stranger's character is unknown.

Technology upends the heuristics that people use to determine whom to trust. In a famous cartoon from the early days of the internet, two dogs are sitting in front of a computer and one explains, "On the Internet, nobody knows you're a dog." Perhaps a more apt line might be, "On the Internet, nobody knows you're a wolf."

Personal Relationships

The law takes a rather cynical view of personal relationships, with courts often refusing to protect trust. In Fourth Amendment cases that involve whether there should be judicial oversight of police surveillance and data gathering, the US Supreme Court has held that when data is shared with third parties, people no longer can expect privacy and must accept the risk of betrayal.[25] Without any oversight, the government can thus deploy agents to pretend to be our friends and spy on us or encourage friends or family members to inform on us.

The government can compel people to breach confidentiality, a technique used in totalitarian societies to turn friends and family members against each other. Although evidentiary privileges protect spouses from being forced to testify against each other, such privileges don't protect the parent-child relationship. In 1998, for example, Special Prosecutor Kenneth Starr was able to compel Monica Lewinsky's mother to testify about private conversations with her daughter.[26]

In civil cases, the law conveys a similarly impoverished conception of privacy in relationships. In one famous case, the car manufacturer General Motors attempted to silence its biggest critic, auto-safety advocate Ralph Nader, unleashing a group of snoopers to probe nearly every corner of Nader's life, interrogating his friends and family in order to find skeletons in his closet. Nader sued, but the court concluded that people have no expectation of trust in others; people must "necessarily assume the risk that a friend or acquaintance in whom he had confided might breach the confidence."[27]

One of the most sinister consequences of totalitarian control is creating a culture in which nobody can be trusted. Although US privacy law protects professional relationships, the law generally fails to appreciate how much personal relationships also matter. Meaningful protection of personal relationships wouldn't mean that the government would be barred from using undercover agents or informants; it would merely require that there be independent judicial oversight of the practice. In civil cases, it would protect the public from the types of techniques GM used against Nader.[28]

Consumer Relationships

The law should also protect people in their relationships with companies. In the Fourth Amendment context, the same third-party doctrine regarding personal relationships applies: even when companies promise confidentiality in their privacy notices, people have no expectation of privacy in data shared with companies.

In civil lawsuits against companies for improper data sharing and use, courts are reluctant to view people's relationships with companies as confidential relationships warranting legal protection.[29] If a doctor were to sell a patient's data to marketers without the patient's consent, the patient could sue for breach of confidentiality; but if a company were to do the same with a customer's data, the customer wouldn't have similar legal recourse.

Some critics of privacy regulation argue that the law shouldn't interfere with the relationships that companies forge with individuals and that the free market will work it out. They claim that if companies do wrong, they'll lose business.

But this view assumes that individuals can discover wrongdoing, which is often hidden and not readily ascertainable. This view also assumes that people can easily go to other companies, but there are often insufficient alternatives, and switching to other companies is difficult and time-consuming. Nor is it clear that other companies will be more trustworthy, as there currently isn't enough information for consumers to determine just how trustworthy companies are. This view also is based on the myth of the law being an interloper on relationships between companies and consumers, as if these relationships exist in some kind of state of nature. In fact, these relationships often are already highly shaped by the law. Companies aren't naturally occurring entities; they are fictitious legal creations to which the law grants special privileges, such as limited liability. Because the law bestows special privileges upon companies, surely it ought to demand greater responsibilities in return.

Fiduciary Relationships and Power

Long ago, I proposed the law of fiduciary relationships as a way to help regulate consumer privacy. For certain relationships very unequal in power, the law imposes special duties on the more powerful party. In what is called a "fiduciary relationship," the law charges a trustee with looking out for the best interests of a beneficiary. Courts have also recognized other relationships as fiduciary ones, such as those between doctors and patients and between lawyers and clients. The special duties in fiduciary relationships include a duty of confidentiality, a duty of loyalty, a duty of care, and a duty to disclose personal interests that could influence one's judgment. The law also protects fiduciary relationships by making third parties liable when they entice or encourage violations of fiduciary duties. In the most famous and eloquent articulation of fiduciary relationships, Justice Benjamin Cardozo wrote: "Not honesty alone, but the punctilio of an honor the most sensitive, is then the standard of behavior."[30]

Overall, the concern animating the law of fiduciary relationships is power. Today, many corporate, governmental, and other entities have enhanced their power over us by collecting and using vast quantities of personal data. Imposing fiduciary duties on these entities would significantly help protect individuals.[31] Fiduciary law is one of the law's wisest creations—a recognition that with great power should come great responsibility. Policymakers should use this body of law in more relationships involving digital technologies.

Power

Control

In the early days of the internet, enthusiasts proclaimed that it should be a radical, unrestricted zone, free from the shackles of regulation and control. Musician and cyber-activist John Perry Barlow issued a famous manifesto: "Governments of the Industrial World, you weary giants of flesh and steel, I come from Cyberspace, the new home of Mind. On behalf of the future, I ask you of the past to leave us alone. You are not welcome among us. You have no sovereignty where we gather."[1] But the internet soon devolved into a darker place—of control, not freedom.[2] This happened not because of regulation but because of a lack of it. In this regulatory void, companies and governments have quickly taken advantage of the internet's vast surveillance capabilities to collect massive quantities of data about individuals and then use the data to control them.

The Panopticon: The Control of Pervasive Surveillance

In 1791, philosopher Jeremy Bentham designed a prison called the "Panopticon," with cells arrayed around a central watchtower—a ruthlessly efficient architecture where fewer guards were needed to watch over prisoners. Prisoners living in constant fear of being watched would become docile, tamed by the ever-present gaze.

Nearly two centuries later, in 1975, philosopher Michel Foucault noted that technology is enabling panoptic power to spread far beyond the concrete walls of prisons. With surveillance technologies, society is building a prison for itself.[3]

In the years since, our devolution into a panoptic society has accelerated. Surveillance cameras continue to multiply like cockroaches, monitored from afar by bleary-eyed bureaucrats. The internet traces everyone's actions online. Data can be recorded about virtually everything people do. As Professors Julie Cohen, Paul Schwartz, and Neil Richards have observed, the effects of our surveillance society stifle free thought and democracy, blunting the edges of expression and intellectual exploration.[4]

At University College London, one can still see Jeremy Bentham—not a statue or portrait but his actual embalmed corpse, displayed rather unceremoniously in a small glass booth. There is a fitting irony to this macabre exhibit: Bentham permanently resides in a panoptic cell.

The Failure of Sousveillance: Control from Below

Some argue that technologies actually enable the people to gain control over large, powerful institutions, and that—through "sousveillance," surveillance from below—individuals can use technology to watch the organizations that watch them. Observers such as David Brin have argued that, instead of pursuing stronger privacy protections, we should aim for a transparent society.[5]

But this view is far too optimistic, for it neglects to account for the unequal power relationships between individuals and large organizations. Individuals lack the power of large organizations to analyze and use data. Indeed, technology rarely equalizes power. Most often, it further empowers the powerful.

The Law Contributes to the Power Imbalance

The law often turns a blind eye to the profound power imbalance between individuals and large organizations. Courts are usually highly sympathetic to organizations processing large quantities of data, and much less sympathetic to people who are injured in the process. Companies often launch new technologies into the world without fully considering the consequences or adequately planning for how to mitigate any harms these technologies might cause. The law generally cheers this innovation and safeguards the corporations' right to profit over the welfare of the individuals they profit from.

Inequality

Technology dangles before us the tantalizing possibility of increasing equality. But instead, technology often amplifies inequality.

Disproportionate Surveillance and Control

The harms of technology aren't equally distributed. Surveillance more systematically targets the poor and marginalized. People in poverty, when they receive financial assistance, are often placed under the oppressive surveillance of the state and forced to "consent" to being monitored and controlled.[6] Racial and religious minorities, being typically viewed as more suspect than other citizens, tend to be singled out for more intrusive watching.[7]

When surveillance is disproportionately used against certain groups of people, it can result in a vicious spiral. Surveillance will catch transgressions, reinforcing the prejudiced view that members of these groups are more likely to transgress, and this will often lead to additional surveillance.

Online attacks and harassment are disproportionately aimed at women and marginalized people. Online mobs dox them, circulate nude images of them, create deep fake porn about them, and threaten them with harm or death, frequently driving them to anxiety, silence, and even breakdown.[8] This appalling behavior is a means of control and oppression; it aims to silence and punish people.

Old and New Forms of Discrimination

Algorithms can exacerbate existing forms of discrimination by more systematically disfavoring certain people. Algorithms can also conceal discrimination by using proxies. For example, instead of disfavoring people based on race or religion, an algorithm might disfavor people based on their address because it is correlated to race or religion. Such discrimination might not be intentional; the algorithm might be reflecting data that is tainted with discrimination.

Algorithms can usher in new forms of discrimination based on characteristics the algorithms identify as salient.[9] These characteristics might not be those traditionally protected by law, such as race, gender, or age, but could instead be traits that have commonly been disfavored, such as being short, overweight, or bald. Even though the law often doesn't protect against such traits, discrimination based on traits that are beyond a person's control is an affront to people's freedom and agency.

Some of the characteristics that algorithms rely upon might seem random; they can be based on uncanny correlations. For example, an algorithm might detect a pattern that people who walk a certain way are more likely to engage in shoplifting or that people who are vegetarian are less likely to be good workers. The result is that new undesirable characteristics will emerge, and they could be used systematically to people's benefit or detriment. People with certain traits or behaviors could be routinely disfavored, losing out on opportunities, being sentenced more harshly, or not being hired. A new form of inequality might arise based on lawful behaviors or traits people can't control—an inequality that is unfair and inimical to freedom.

The Technology-Neutrality Myth

Algorithmic decisions often turn out to be biased, since they are highly data-driven and the data they are trained on is frequently riddled with bias. This problem is often obscured by the technology-neutrality myth, in which technology is wrongly viewed as cleansed of bias. Even when an algorithm itself isn't biased, the algorithm's output can reflect bias in the data. If the ills of society are reflected in its data, the data may poison everything it touches. As Sandra Mayson aptly says, "Bias in, bias out."[10]

One of the main problems with technology is the way that people think about it. Rarely will a technology rise above the society in which it is deployed. Instead of curing the ills of society, technology tends to turn up the volume. The technology-neutrality myth not only cloaks this problem but makes it worse by offering technology as a cure when it is actually worsening the disease. The law must look beyond this myth and shift its focus from intentions to effects, since even technology created without an intent to treat people unequally must be held responsible for its effects.[11]

Identification

Identification links people to data in dossiers about them, which threatens the anonymity people enjoy in many daily activities. Identification makes it hard to avoid being watched and tracked.

Systematic Control

Identification is an essential step in the systematic control of populations. If people can be readily identified, it is far easier for the government to monitor them. Identification facilitates the ability of governments to oppress, detain, or eliminate disfavored individuals, a common technique of totalitarian societies.

Over the last hundred years, identification has transformed from the visible and occasional (physical markings, branding, mutilation, scarlet letters) to the concealed and efficient (identification numbers, databases, biometrics). When identification is systematic and secret, the risk of abuse becomes far greater.[12]

The Challenge of De-Identification

Technology challenges the ability to de-identify data, a key method of protecting privacy.[13] There is a spectrum of risk regarding the re-identification of data.[14] Much of the equation about the risk of re-identification depends upon an evolving variable—the personal data that already exists in identified form. When so much identified personal data is already available, it is easy to link it to de-identified data. Much like the languages on the Rosetta Stone, de-identified data can be compared to existing identified data. If there is enough overlap, the de-identified data can then be re-identified.

The Law's Contribution to the Problem

Governments often develop identification systems for their own interests, which are not always aligned with what is best for individuals. For example, the US Social Security number (SSN) has been misused by organizations and today can expose individuals to grave risks of identity theft.[15] Used by organizations as means of identification or passwords, SSNs are routinely exposed in data breaches or mistakenly released by the government in public records.

Since the law fails to restrict the sale of SSNs, companies are permitted to sell them. Nor does the law prohibit the use of SSNs as a way to authenticate identity. Organizations use people's SSNs like passwords; if someone knows your SSN, then organizations presume that the person is you. Identity thieves can readily exploit this practice by finding people's SSNs and using them to perpetrate fraud.

Biometric Identification and Facial Recognition

Organizations have recently been shifting to a reliance on biometric data—information about body parts and characteristics, such as fingerprints, eyes, voice, and gait—for identification. Though this shift has promise for more precise identification, it carries underappreciated risks. Passwords can be changed; biometrics can't. Thus, if biometric data becomes compromised, there's no fix. Unfortunately, establishing strong and reliable data security remains an elusive goal, and most organizations have suffered many data breaches.

For a long time, facial recognition technology (a form of biometric identification) sputtered, with multiple failed attempts to take off. These failures were typically the result of poor accuracy rates, though some initial attempts were abandoned when companies concluded that the technology was too potentially harmful. But then a twenty-eight-year-old programmer, who had previously constructed frivolous games and apps, founded Clearview AI and began scraping billions of photos from the internet without people's consent to create a facial-recognition system capable of high accuracy. Law-enforcement agencies around the world eagerly adopted his technology.[16]

Facial-recognition technology, if deployed widely, can eliminate the possibility for any semblance of physical obscurity. In one incident, the company that owned Madison Square Garden used facial recognition to identify lawyers who had sued it.[17] When the lawyers entered the building, security guards kicked them out, in a petty act of retaliation.

The Clearview AI story illustrates how new technology can be developed readily without even a modicum of concern about its societal effects. All that matters is that it be cool and profitable. While some companies might forbear to pursue such a project because of ethical concerns, there will be others that won't.

The law addressing the problems of biometric identification remains woefully underdeveloped. Only a few laws, such as the Illinois Biometric Information Privacy Act, require consent to collect biometric information. But even the Illinois law doesn't apply to the government, and there is scant oversight or accountability for the ways in which lawfully obtained biometric identification can be used, especially by the government. The failure is not due to the technology being too new and complex—an excuse policymakers often invoke for their sluggish responses to technological innovation—since biometric identification has actually been around for a long time. There are many obvious steps the law could take to address the problems of biometric information, such as meaningful control and oversight on the collection and use of this information, not just by companies but also by the government. As is often the case, the law's failure stems from a lack of political will.

Cost

Technology today enables anyone, at hardly any cost, to create and spread information. Though cost used to serve as a limiting factor to how much data one could store, this limit is melting away, and today organizations can inexpensively amass and store massive quantities of personal data.

The Decline of Traditional Gatekeepers and Privacy Norms

In recent decades, ordinary people have been given unprecedented power to communicate widely, and amateurs now are capable of producing videos and podcasts and social-media postings that zoom around the world. The results are troubling.

In the past, mainstream media served as gatekeepers to communicating to the wider public. Despite their hunger for gossipy stories, the mainstream media mostly adhered to privacy norms and professional standards. But with modern technology, what constitutes "the media" is no longer limited to mainstream entities. Anyone can now cheaply produce communications with a sheen of good production values.[18] As a result, media norms are becoming more fractured and divergent. The old-fashioned slogan "All the news that's fit to print" has been replaced with "Anything goes."

The Threat to Data Minimization

Low cost enables organizations to vacuum up vast quantities of personal data and store it indefinitely. Many privacy laws are trying to rein in the drive to gather and store data by imposing a principle of "data minimization"—a requirement to collect only the minimum amount of data necessary for one's purpose and to stop retaining it after that purpose has been achieved. But the data-minimization provisions in many laws are more decorative than meaningful. Their provisions often amount to vague exhortations to avoid gorging on data—akin to advising diners at a grand buffet with mouthwatering food to please eat lightly. And because data minimization often involves judgment calls, it is tricky to enforce; as a result, regulators focus most of their attention on clearer and simpler violations of the law.

More Power, Less Responsibility

As Mustafa Suleyman notes, "Almost every foundational technology ever invented, from pickaxes to plows, pottery to photography, phones to planes, and everything in between, follows a single, seemingly immutable law: it gets cheaper and easier to use, and ultimately it proliferates, far and wide."[19] This proliferation of technology puts it in the hands of many people who lack the judgment, morality, or maturity to use it responsibly.

Powerful surveillance technologies are now readily available for purchase. Hackers don't need to learn to code; they can buy hacking kits that contain everything they need. With AI-powered technology, users can create deepfake images and videos that can make it hard to distinguish truth from fiction.[20] This "great cheapening" has left individuals and organizations with more power and less accountability.

Where cost no longer restrains such activity, the law must step in. Otherwise, we will end up in a world where many wield dangerous power without adequate responsibility.

Scale

With digital technologies, personal data can be processed on a massive scale. Technology amplifies and extends, enabling unprecedented surveillance and data gathering. Systems of responsibility and accountability haven't caught up.

Scaling Without Responsibility

With the assistance of technology, organizations often behave like teenagers who have matured faster physically than psychologically. The story is often the same: A startup technology company finds sudden success and scales up rapidly. The company ignores privacy risks, causes harm to countless people, and eventually attracts the attention of regulators. The regulators give the company a slap, which causes a temporary sting but rarely significant pain. The company then matures, hires a compliance team, and starts to take privacy at least somewhat more seriously.

This story occurs again and again, because the law allows it. Companies gain more by growing fast and transgressing, then apologizing after getting caught and paying a modest penalty. Rarely are the consequences of regulatory sanctions so severe as to cancel all the benefits a company managed to gain from its violations. *Better to ask for forgiveness than permission* is a maxim that such companies know well.[21]

Companies rarely are able to cover the costs of the harm they create at scale. When a company has billions of users, causing small harms for each user can aggregate to a massive amount of total harm. The law recognizes and addresses severe harm done to one person much more readily than smaller harms dispersed among many people.

The Law's Failure to Demand Accountability

The law struggles to address problems of scale because it is reluctant to demand accountability. In one case, a credit-reporting company falsely stated that a person went bankrupt. The court rejected the person's lawsuit because "mistakes can happen" when a company processes an "enormous volume of information"[22]—essentially blessing a business model that prioritizes scale and profit over avoiding errors that may cause individual injury.

Courts routinely sympathize with Big Data companies, protecting business models that involve processing massive quantities of personal data on hundreds of millions of people without internalizing the damage caused by their activities. Until companies are held accountable and forced to absorb the full costs of their activities, they will continue to cause harm.

Harm

The law often won't intervene to protect privacy unless people are harmed. Harm from privacy violations has long been difficult to recognize because it is often intangible and tends not to involve blood, pain, or death. As a result, the law has struggled in its attempts to protect privacy.

A Gatekeeper to the Law

Harm often serves as a watchword in privacy cases. When people want to sue for a privacy violation, many laws require that they show they were harmed. In countless cases, courts have refused to recognize privacy harms that don't cause tangible injuries.[23]

In US federal courts, people must establish "standing" in order to sue—that is, must demonstrate a concrete injury that isn't speculative. In one case, *TransUnion v. Ramirez*, a credit-reporting company wrongly listed people as potential terrorists based on a mere name match with suspects on a terrorist watch list. The company's shoddy procedure was a clear violation of the federal Fair Credit Reporting Act (FCRA). But despite this egregious violation of the law, the US Supreme Court barred many people from suing, reasoning that they weren't harmed because the information hadn't yet been disclosed.[24] In matters of privacy and technology, cases like *Ramirez* are unfortunately legion.

Many privacy violations involve breached promises, unwanted advertising, manipulation, and other harms that are hard to quantify and are not physical. Many have downstream effects that will not manifest until long after the expiration of the statute of limitations, beyond which people are barred from suing.

Aggregation of Small Harms

Many privacy harms, such as receiving unwanted advertisements or emails, are small in isolation, each instance representing no more than an annoyance or minuscule inconvenience. But with modern technology and the multitude of organizations that collect, use, and disclose personal data, these small harms can add up for each individual as well as for society.

The law works well when addressing a few actors that cause significant and visceral harm. It struggles when harm is dispersed and caused by thousands of actors.

Societal Harm

Though the law often focuses intently on individual harm, privacy harms tend to be societal in nature. However, many courts won't recognize societal harm. In one case, Melody Stoops sued a company for illegally making telemarketing calls in violation of the Telephone Consumer Protection Act (TCPA).[25] The Act prohibits companies from making unsolicited calls to people who are on a do-not-call registry or who have asked the company not to call them again. The court, however, threw out her lawsuit. Stoops' mission was to catch and punish violators, so she brought many cases. The court reasoned that she wasn't harmed because she actually wanted to receive these illegal calls in order to catch violators, so she didn't suffer an injury.[26]

The court was wrong to dismiss this case. Melody Stoops was, in essence, setting up a sting operation, catching companies that were flagrantly breaking the law. She was trying to stop the societal harm the TCPA was passed to combat—the constant bombardment of unwanted phone calls. The fact that she invited harm upon herself by buying multiple cell phones doesn't mean that she wasn't harmed. By attempting to hold companies liable for violations, Stoops was helping the law achieve its goals. Without people like Stoops, companies can get away with breaking the law because only a few people have the time and knowledge to sue. But, as courts commonly do, this court took the side of the company that flagrantly violated the law rather than that of the person trying to hold the company accountable.

The Many Types of Privacy Harm

Since privacy is not one thing but many different things, it follows that not all privacy harms are the same. In my work with Professor Danielle Citron, we identified many different types of privacy harm. While traditional harms include physical, economic, and reputational harm, many privacy harms are different. Some are psychological, such as emotional distress or disruption of one's peace of mind. Others involve autonomy, by restricting or unduly influencing people's choices through coercion, manipulation, failure to adequately inform, thwarting expectations, using personal data without permission, and inhibiting engagement in lawful activities. Still other harms involve discrimination, entrenching inequality or creating disadvantage based on certain characteristics. Privacy violations can impair important personal and professional relationships.[27]

The law generally handles physical, economic, and reputational harms well, but it struggles with the other types of harms, often ignoring or trivializing them. Until the law modernizes its understanding of harm to include the deleterious effects of modern digital technologies, it will be hobbled in protecting privacy.

Since regulatory agencies are limited in budget and staff and thus constrained to pursuing only a fraction of the ongoing violations, private litigation is an essential tool for enforcing laws. So when courts slam their doors on lawsuits, they disable a vital factor in the development of the law and one of the most effective means of enforcement.[28]

Vulnerability

If the digital world were physical, it wouldn't consist of sturdy buildings in an idyllic land of rolling hills and flowers. It would instead be a shantytown of rickety shacks with gaping holes, missing doors, and broken windows, and with bandits scurrying about like rats. The digital world is a treacherous place; danger is embedded in its very design, and the law often heightens that danger.

Architectures of Vulnerability

Our current data ecosystem—the elaborate weblike network through which personal data circulates—is woefully insecure. It is not only clandestine and inscrutable but also vulnerable and exploitable. Our data is hoarded by gigantic companies and government entities and stored in vast repositories, where it is often inadequately guarded. Hackers readily nibble their way into these data stores.

The internet wasn't built with security in mind, and attempts to graft security onto its wobbly architecture have struggled and often faltered. Identity thieves can obtain people's personal data with moderate effort and use it to break into accounts or commit fraud in people's names. Hackers can easily impersonate people, spoof emails, and release malware.

The law is partly responsible for creating this vulnerable environment. For example, companies can grant credit easily and quickly—almost instantly. Credit cards can be obtained online or through the mail by providing only a small amount of personal information, much of which an identity thief can find. Making credit cards convenient to obtain and profitable for their issuer has increased their vulnerability to fraud. Because of such vulnerabilities, the law often fails to hold companies responsible for the harms caused to fraud victims. More broadly, the law has structured the data ecosystem to allow companies to externalize their costs.[29]

Insecure technologies are legion. The market doesn't incentivize security; people buy devices and software based on price and functionality, and most consumers don't know enough to assess security. For example, most home-security systems and baby cameras on the market are outrageously insecure, but few buyers are able to determine which products are secure and which are not. The law fails to hold the makers of these products liable for the damage they cause, nor does it adequately hold responsible the platforms on which insecure technologies are marketed and sold.[30]

Individuals using these technologies and sharing their personal data are left on their own to assess the security risks, even though they lack the knowledge and expertise to do so.

Risk and Harm

In today's digital world, people must live precariously. Organizations can significantly increase people's risk of being harmed yet evade accountability themselves. For example, companies typically suffer data breaches in part because of poor security, but when people sue because their data was compromised, many courts fail to recognize harm and dismiss the cases.[31] The lesson to companies is that they don't have to internalize the costs that they would rather slough off on individuals.

As one example, a medical institution lost a laptop with the health data of about 7,500 patients, as well as boxes with pathology reports and medical diagnoses. The court, however, concluded that the patients weren't harmed because they had not been subjected to fraud,[32] and ignored their emotional distress over the exposure of their health data and their increased risk of future harm.

Failing to Address Data Security Holistically

The law often focuses obsessively on data breaches. The law becomes involved only after a breach occurs, and it usually pummels the organizations that suffered the breach. But data breaches are typically the final chapter in a long story involving an ensemble of characters and entities that all play a role: designers of insecure devices and software, platforms that distribute insecure ads or apps, and facilitators who create vulnerabilities for hackers to exploit. The law rarely distributes responsibility, instead focusing way too much on the organizations affected. This myopic focus fails to address much of the problem. Ironically, if the law focused less on data breaches, it would be more effective at preventing them.[33]

Accountability

In the world of technology, accountability is often lacking. Accountability means exercising conscientiousness over one's actions, being mindful of the consequences, and anticipating and preventing situations that might result in harm. Accountability also involves being held responsible for one's actions, being transparent with the public, and internalizing one's costs rather than passing them on to others. When technology undermines accountability in certain circumstances, the law typically fails to hold its creators and users responsible.

Anonymity and Accountability

Social-media companies regularly unleash technologies that lead to people's being less accountable for their behavior. When things go wrong, the companies disavow responsibility, pointing to their users as the ones to blame.

With the internet, people are able to communicate anonymously, cloaking their real identities. Anonymity enables people to be free to express themselves and explore unpopular ideas without fear of reprisal or ostracism.[34] But it also enables people to say venomous things and do vile deeds. Professor Danielle Citron has vividly chronicled how hordes of online trolls can spew the most cruel and toxic comments and threats.[35]

When online attackers are unmasked, the true horror is revealed: Many of them are not miscreants in basements but instead are seemingly normal people. Removing accountability is certainly revealing; some might say that a lack of accountability shows us who people truly are. But it isn't quite that simple. Instead, accountability actually shapes people and improves their behavior; lack of accountability has the opposite effect.

Technology Exceptionalism

Creators of technology are often given a special pass by the law. Online platforms often disclaim responsibility for people's behavior, with the law facilitating their lack of accountability by granting them immunity from lawsuits. Section 230 of the US Communications Decency Act (CDA) provides online platforms with special protections that the print and broadcast media lack, stating that "No provider or user of an interactive computer service shall be treated as the publisher or speaker of any information provided by another information content provider."[36]

The text of Section 230 is narrowly focused, but courts have interpreted it broadly as a huge grant of immunity to platforms for the speech of their users.[37] Though Section 230 wasn't written to eliminate liability for distributing information known to be defamatory or invasive of privacy, courts have interpreted it to wipe out such liability.[38]

Section 230 as currently interpreted allows online platforms to ignore people's pleas for help when they are injured by posts containing vile harassment, vicious lies, or intimate photos or secrets.[39] Instead of encouraging accountability, the law facilitates the opposite; online platforms are even left free to solicit and facilitate harmful posts. This lack of accountability has spawned thousands of sites that encourage users to post nonconsensual naked photos of victims.[40]

In its zeal to protect free speech, the law fails to acknowledge that the values of free speech are not furthered by threats, harassment, or nonconsensual nude photos.

Platforms are by no means the only dangerous digital environment. Many websites, apps, and software have harmful bugs, faulty designs, and vulnerabilities that can expose users to harm. Yet the law rarely steps in.

Many tech companies cheerfully proclaim how they "break things," unleashing new technologies on society without much thought about the consequences. But breaking things isn't inherent in technology—it's an ethos. Part of the swagger of technology companies comes from not worrying about the consequences.

PART III

POWER, LAW, AND ACCOUNTABILITY

Technology is posing tremendous challenges for privacy in a multitude of ways. Privacy law finds itself in a perpetual struggle to keep up with the dizzying pace of changing technologies.

Technology allows us to sweeten the bitter plan the universe has for us. But the universe can be a sadistic comedian. It rarely gives without taking. It tantalizes us with wondrous things that can also damage us. Solve one problem, and the solution leads to another problem. After every technological advance, the universe chuckles and sows sinister seeds of future hazards into the victory.

Will we ever transcend the cruel paradoxes and ironies posed by technology? I doubt it. But we mustn't give up hope: Even if we can't win, we must at least try not to lose.

It's not yet time to eulogize privacy. The law can keep privacy alive, but it will take hard work and considerable rethinking. In the pages that follow, I explain what will be necessary.

Privacy and Power

Privacy is about power.[1] To be effective, the law must respond to this fundamental fact. The problems discussed in this book, although exacerbated by technology, are largely caused by people exercising power. And they are architectural in nature: they emerge from the way that organizations, the data ecosystem, and social relationships are structured.

Organizations are creatures of law, which bestows upon them special powers and privileges. Thus, the burden of establishing accountability is ultimately on the law, which must shape the appropriate structure and set the right incentives. Far too often, the law fails in these basic functions. In many cases, the law itself has created or contributed to the problems by the way it has structured the digital economy, by the incentives it has created and the activities it has facilitated.

On the front lines of technological change are the corporations and institutions that drive the change. These organizations can indeed act badly, and they are often demonized. But castigating them as evil mostly distracts from the true roots of the problems. Although agencies, organizations, and corporations aren't inherently evil, they're not inherently good either: they do what they are incentivized to do. A government spy agency will zealously engage in surveillance, and a corporation will seek to maximize profits. Organizations rarely stop themselves when they really want to do something. Expecting voluntary virtue and restraint from them is about as futile as hoping that a shark will forgo eating seals and become a vegetarian. Instead of blaming them for it, we should blame the law for enabling it.

Many privacy laws still naively rely upon self-regulation, along with a thin veneer of enforcement. But self-regulation hasn't worked and can never work. Far too much policy is crafted on a hope and a prayer that organizations will behave in chivalrous ways rather than zealously pursuing their interests.

The law frequently gives technology a pass, rarely holding creators and users of technology accountable. And as a result, agencies and corporations may lack sufficient incentives to address the problems they have created.

But accountability works. Hold people and companies accountable, and they will behave better. Set up the right incentives and the right behavior will ensue. As the investor Charlie Munger famously said, "Show me the incentive, and I'll show you the outcome."[2]

In *The Coming Wave*, Mustafa Suleyman, a founder of two AI companies, argues that new technologies always become cheaper and proliferate. They become part of the fabric of life, and they spread in waves that are impossible to stop.[3] Although the law can't stop technology, the law still is able to steer it.

Arguments that law will stifle innovation ironically underestimate the power of technology. If the law poses a challenge, technology will likely find a solution; after all, technology is designed to solve problems. The law should challenge technology rather than be driven by it.

Tech companies constantly tell us two narratives. To the world they proudly proclaim, "Anything is possible—behold the power of innovation!" But when presented with modest regulation, they protest, "Regulation is too hard to comply with—we can't do it!"

Why can't companies innovate to find ways to follow the law? Because innovating in order to comply with regulation is less intoxicating than innovating for profit, glory, or power. For companies, this is a matter not of *can't do* but rather of *don't want to do*. Calls to free technology from the shackles of law in order to facilitate innovation are really demands to defer to powerful companies that want to do whatever they please.

Currently, the law has created an environment for reckless technological growth. If the law incentivized thoughtfulness, morality, and care, we'd see a different kind of innovation, one that was responsible and less potentially harmful, one that incorporated protecting privacy into its goals rather than treating privacy concerns as an impediment.

Regulating technology involves imagining the future and understanding power. The law can naively hope that virtue or restraint will do the work of regulation, that organizations will just do the right thing, that the lion will lay down with the lamb. In reality, however, power rarely yields to anything except power.

The Law's Role

What should the law do to protect us from the harms that technology can cause? Over the past century, privacy laws have been sprouting up at a remarkable pace, which is intensifying each decade. Though law typically moves at the pace of a tortoise, privacy law is racing at the speed of a hare.

The EU's General Data Protection Regulation (GDPR) is a terrific law, but it is just an early step in a long journey. Many of its provisions unfortunately place too much of the onus on individuals to self-manage their privacy, a shortcoming I will discuss later on.

Privacy laws around the world have often copied the GDPR, but in weaker forms and with missing pieces. The United States lacks a comprehensive federal privacy law like the GDPR. Though there are countless narrow federal laws and an emerging number of state consumer privacy laws, most of them are inadequate; even worse, many are heading in the wrong direction.

The Canard of Self-Regulation

In the early days of the internet, as concerns about privacy mounted, the technology industry aggressively pushed self-regulation as the solution. Technology companies would post a privacy notice to inform people how their data was being collected, used, and transferred, promising that data would only be used in limited ways and would be protected with reasonable security measures. But these promises were hollow. A tour through enforcement cases and news stories reveals egregious violations by nearly all the largest technology companies. Still, as the internet blossomed in the 1990s and early

2000s, companies generally succeeded in convincing policymakers that self-regulation could work.

As US privacy law began to develop, the approach taken was largely self-regulatory—an approach known as "notice-and-choice." The laws typically required companies to post a privacy notice and offer users at least some kind of choice. In some cases, users could opt out of certain (though rarely all) uses or disclosures of their data. But often the only "choice" people had was to take it or leave it, either accepting the company's practices or not doing business with it at all.

The notice-and-choice approach, which persists in many laws to this day, essentially amounts to self-regulation, with a thin varnish of enforcement to lend it the appearance of legitimacy. In the mid-1990s, the Federal Trade Commission added some teeth to privacy notices by interpreting a broken promise of privacy by a corporation as an illegal "deceptive" trade practice.[1] But it remains easy for companies to navigate around this. It turns out that hardly anybody reads privacy notices and that only a handful of people opt out; and companies' promises are typically so vague that they are effectively left free to do whatever they want.[2]

In the end, self-regulation doesn't work. This shouldn't be surprising: the incentives are all wrong, and everyone knows that the fox can't guard the henhouse. Though critics have thoroughly condemned the notice-and-choice approach,[3] privacy law in the United States still clings to it. Beginning with the California Consumer Privacy Act (CCPA) in 2018, a wave of state consumer-privacy laws has followed the notice-and-choice approach. While the laws have tried to ensure that the notice must be conspicuous, research shows that people don't read such language no matter how conspicuous it is.[4]

The Impossibility of Self-Help

Can individuals protect themselves on their own? Many commentators point to measures that people can take to protect their privacy: being cautious about sharing personal data, encrypting communications, opting out of behavioral marketing, and so on. But these measures are little better than rearranging deck chairs on the Titanic;

they aren't quite negligible, but they mostly give people the illusion that they are in control when they actually aren't. Most data gathering and surveillance are surreptitious and far beyond people's ability to control. Despite even the most diligent efforts to protect personal data and the stingiest practices in sharing it, individuals can't stop most organizations from using massive quantities of their data.

Living off the grid is impractical; people can't escape digital technology today, when its tentacles are deeply entwined with nearly all facets of life. And privacy can't be protected by individuals alone; for meaningful privacy protection, the law must do more than punt the ball to individuals – it must hold organizations accountable.

The Futility of Individual Control

Most privacy laws around the world aim to give individuals control over their data. Laws provide people with a right to obtain information about the data collected about them as well as rights to access, correct, and delete their data. Laws often focus heavily on individual consent.[5]

Intuitively, the idea of giving individuals greater control is understandable. If the privacy problems posed by digital technologies disempower people, leaving them helpless in a world where they've lost control of their data, then the obvious response is to give them back that control. Unfortunately, this response has failed.[6]

As mentioned earlier, I've found the work of Franz Kafka to aptly capture the problems of privacy in today's digital age. In many of his novels and stories, Kafka's characters often surrender what little power they have, even when they aren't being coerced.[7] Victims often blame themselves for their victimization; people often willingly submit to authority.

Kafka's dark view of human nature captures many realities that privacy law must address. The law often assumes that if people are given options and are protected from deception and manipulation, they will make wise choices in their self-interest. But this optimism is naive. With digital technologies, people readily surrender their privacy, even when doing so seems contrary to their own interests. Companies don't need to coerce when they can seduce. People enthusiastically embrace new technologies that strip them of their data, bringing these technologies into their homes and attaching them to their bodies. When they suffer harm as a result, they often blame themselves.[8]

The law tries relentlessly to give people control, but they often give it right back. Rather than truly empowering individuals, the law creates a façade of empowerment, ironically leading to further disempowerment.

In today's world of AI, the algorithms that power automated decisions are far too complex for users to understand. To be able to truly assess their risks, users must themselves become data scientists and must also be able to review the enormous quantities of data used to train the algorithms, which isn't feasible.

Although offering individuals control over their data is a well-meaning impulse, privacy law has taken a wrong turn in trying to do so. The law should instead attempt to bring the collection, use, and disclosure of personal data under control.

The Failure of Privacy Self-Management

The current regulatory approach for protecting privacy involves what I refer to as "privacy self-management": that is, the law provides people with a set of rights to enable them to weigh the costs and benefits of the collection, use, or disclosure of their information. People's consent legitimizes nearly any form of collection, use, and disclosure of their personal data.[9]

Unfortunately, privacy self-management doesn't provide meaningful control. Empirical and social-science research has undermined key assumptions about how people make decisions regarding their data, the very assumptions that underpin and legitimize the privacy self-management model.[10] People don't read privacy notices, can't understand them if they do, and rarely make informed decisions about their privacy.

A series of structural problems impedes users in any attempts to appropriately self-manage their privacy. There are too many entities collecting and using personal data to make it feasible for individuals to manage their privacy separately with each entity. Many privacy harms are the result of an aggregation of pieces of data over time by different entities. It is virtually impossible for people to weigh the costs and benefits of revealing data without an understanding of its potential downstream uses. In addition, privacy self-management addresses privacy in a series of isolated transactions guided by particular individuals, whereas privacy costs and benefits should properly be assessed not at the individual level but cumulatively and holistically at the societal level.[11]

Privacy self-management is a vast, complex, and never-ending project that doesn't scale. Though privacy regulation often seeks to give people more capacity for privacy self-management, doing so won't protect privacy effectively. Problems involving technology and privacy can't be tackled at the individual level; instead, they require the law to make bold changes about how the data ecosystem is structured. Privacy law needs to focus on regulating the architecture that structures the way information is collected, used, and transferred.

Privacy and Milk

When you go to the supermarket and shop for milk, you can rest assured that it's not going to kill you. You can focus on taste and price with no need to research the safety of the farms where the milk originated.

In the days before food safety regulation in the United States, food was often laced with disgusting and even poisonous substances. Coffee might be mixed with sawdust; brown sugar could contain ground insects; spices might be partly brick dust or charcoal; candy and food dyes often contained lead. Milk was especially dangerous: milk producers would mix in formaldehyde to preserve milk and sweeten it when it turned sour, with the result that hundreds of babies died from poisoning.[12]

Today, we take so much for granted: We can eat without worrying that our food is toxic; we can use products without worrying they will explode; we can enter buildings without worrying they will collapse. Yet with digital technologies, we're mostly on our own. The law doesn't watch our back; though we've won a few rights in the realm of privacy, we're largely expected to fend for ourselves, even though we lack the expertise to do so.

Throughout the recent history of technology, the same stories, the same myths, and the same faulty arguments have been trotted out. A common narrative is that people are to blame: When technology causes harm, blame its users.

This tactic was formerly used with automobiles. As car accident deaths rose to an unprecedented level of carnage, the strategy of the carmakers was to advance narratives to blame bad drivers. Of course, there were plenty of bad drivers, but focusing on the drivers shifted attention away from unsafe cars. When the law finally demanded safer cars, cars quickly became much safer.

The same story played out with workplace safety. To distract attention from abominable workplace conditions, companies continued to blame injuries and deaths on careless workers until regulation finally intervened.[13]

With digital technologies and privacy, the blame-the-individual strategy persists. People are blamed for undermining their privacy by sharing their data on social media, even though the platforms they use are designed to encourage them to do just that. Users are blamed for not reading privacy notices, not accessing and correcting their data, or not opting out. Though these tasks require a good deal of work and are impossible to do at scale, individuals' failure to act allows companies to accuse them of not caring about these issues. People are blamed when they allow companies to collect and use their data, even when users say they actually care a lot about privacy. As I noted earlier, this phenomenon has been dubbed the "privacy paradox." If people cared more about their privacy, some argue, then they wouldn't share their data so readily. But companies use many techniques to encourage and even manipulate people into sharing their data.

Data security is likewise treated as the responsibility of ordinary users. Though it is true that many data breaches are due to human error, the security advice that users are given is often so difficult or inconvenient to follow that failure is foreordained. For example, we are asked to concoct long and complex passwords, to use different passwords for each website, and to change them frequently. But doing this strains human cognitive ability, especially when an individual may have hundreds of accounts, and we often fail spectacularly at it, usually by choosing inadequate passwords. The near-impossible is being asked of people, and they are being blamed when they fail.[14]

The law continues to place privacy and data security in the hands of people who lack the ability to protect themselves. Perhaps if we remember the stories of milk and cars, we can learn from all the casualties. Just as we buy milk today without concern it will poison us, we should be able to use digital technologies with confidence that we won't be harmed.

How the Law Should Develop

Privacy law in the Digital Age today is like volcanic magma: it is still quite malleable and hasn't yet cooled. Unlike other bodies of law that have long since hardened—where change now occurs only through slow processes, like rock being sculpted by rain and wind—privacy law continues to simmer and steam, a molten mass that retains the potential to develop in different ways.

Many legal theories have barely been tested in courts. Countless regulatory ideas and techniques have been tried out haphazardly but rarely systematically. A myriad of questions have yet to be answered in the law. For many issues, ideas for an effective regulatory approach remain elusive. We know more about what doesn't work than what does. But progress is still being made.

Although clear and simple laws are generally hailed as an ideal, when it comes to privacy and technology I lean toward a contrarian view: laws that are messy and uncertain actually can be much better. Though the process of working with and applying such laws can be somewhat awkward, the results tend to be far superior.

The Virtues of Open-Ended Laws

When laws are too tightly tethered to existing technology, they lose their flexibility. Technology changes over time, and the application of the law often becomes inconsistent with the original values the law was trying to advance. Fitting new technologies into antiquated laws becomes a major challenge.

For example, the US Electronic Communications Privacy Act (ECPA), enacted in 1986 to regulate electronic surveillance, is a highly detailed law written to deal with the technology of its time. Nearly forty years later, not having been substantially updated, ECPA has become ill-suited to its task. Its levels of protection turn on distinctions that don't mean much today, such as whether communications are traveling through a wire or other means, whether they take the form of emails or phone calls or texts, whether email messages have been read or unread, and whether communications are surveilled contemporaneously or after they occurred. Its scaffolding is wrapped so tightly around the technology of its time that courts struggle to apply it to modern communications technology. Its application now seems to rely on contingencies and arbitrary distinctions rather than coherent policy.

The lesson we should learn from such legislation is that laws should focus less on how technology *works* and more on what technology *does*. Laws in this realm work better when they are more open-ended and not tethered to specific technologies. The US Video Privacy Protection Act (VPPA), for example, wisely defines its scope of coverage to cover not just video tapes (the reigning video technology when the law was passed in 1988) but also "similar audio visual materials."[1] This language has allowed the VPPA to adapt to address technology as it has evolved from video tapes to DVDs to online streaming. To deal with changing technology, the law must be flexible. It must provide room to grow.

Reframing for a Broader View

The Fourth Amendment to the US Constitution is our primary protection against law-enforcement surveillance and information gathering. Though the Fourth Amendment doesn't directly prohibit such activities, it requires oversight and sets limits by requiring law-enforcement officials to obtain a warrant supported by probable cause and issued by a court.

But the Fourth Amendment only protects when data gathering by law enforcement falls within its scope, and the US Supreme Court has long struggled with determining when Fourth Amendment protections apply. Early on, the Court held that there had to be a physical trespass for the Fourth Amendment to apply. In one case, *Olmstead v. United States* (1928), known as the "case of the whispering wires," law enforcement had wiretapped a person's phone calls and obtained evidence of a crime. The Court concluded that because the wiretapping was done outside the person's home, it wasn't a physical trespass.[2] Justice Louis Brandeis dissented and argued that, in clinging to an antiquated requirement of a physical trespass, the Court was being naive about new technologies. Nearly forty years later, the Court reversed *Olmstead*, holding that the Fourth Amendment protects privacy and that it applies whenever privacy is invaded.[3] Subsequently, however, the Court adopted a narrow conception of privacy and rejected many cases involving invasive surveillance and data gathering.[4]

To better protect privacy, Fourth Amendment law should move away from focusing so much on privacy.[5] Indeed, the language of the Fourth Amendment doesn't mention "physical trespass" or "privacy"; it only speaks generally in terms of "unreasonable searches and seizures." Instead of looking to a conception of privacy, which the Court has viewed quite narrowly, the Court should focus on what is "unreasonable." Any government data-gathering activity that creates risk of abuses, potential chilling effects, or other problems should be regarded as unreasonable if it is not subjected to oversight and legal guardrails. The Fourth Amendment should be understood not as primarily an individualistic protection but as a fortification against excessive government power. Protecting privacy is a dimension of this larger goal. Ironically, focusing less directly on privacy will result in more comprehensive protection of privacy.

Similarly, in order to protect against data breaches, data security law should move away from obsessing about such breaches. Once a data breach happens, the law typically starts flogging the organization that suffered the breach. And almost always, the organization could have done better; bungles and blunders occur constantly. But as I wrote in a book with Woodrow Hartzog, the law ignores many other actors that play a pivotal role in causing data breaches. Breaches are just the tip of the iceberg, and the law must look far beyond them to the entire data ecosystem.[6]

Privacy involves complex issues that are best considered by looking beyond the immediate instances in front of us. Far too often, the law turns out to be too narrowly focused. When it comes to privacy, the law has been much too individualistic; rarely looking beyond the case at hand, it typically focuses mainly on individuals and fails to address the bigger picture.

The Danger of Ossification

A major danger is that privacy law will harden, become ossified, and cease to develop. To have any chance of keeping up with technology, it must continue to evolve.

The history of privacy torts in the United States demonstrates both the success of legal dynamism and the perils of ossification. Recall the article I discussed earlier, "The Right to Privacy" (1890), by Samuel Warren and Louis Brandeis,[7] which raised concerns about technology's threats to privacy and called for the law to address privacy violations. One important protection the authors proposed were torts—laws that enable individuals to sue others, in this case those who violate their privacy. This article eventually led to legal responses in nearly all fifty states, and it has been hailed as the "most influential law review article of all."[8] But it was hardly influential for a long time.

Not much had been written about privacy law before 1890. Indeed, this was the first piece on the topic for the authors themselves, who had previously written two articles on the obscure subject of pond law. For more than ten years following its publication, not much really happened in response. Though one court recognized a right to privacy, that decision was reversed a few years later.[9] By 1900, the article looked like quite a flop. It had hardly had an impact, the laws remained unchanged, and the authors themselves had written nothing more on privacy.

In 1902, in *Roberson v. Rochester Folding Box Company*, lawyers cited the article in a lawsuit against a company that used a woman's image on an advertisement without her consent. The court held that the right to privacy had no basis in the law.[10] Another setback.

But the case sparked public attention, and the court's decision was panned by the news media and other commentators. A year later, the New York legislature enacted a statute to allow people to sue for invasion of privacy. Warren and Brandeis finally had their first victory.

During the mid-20th century, the influence of their article began to be felt widely. Privacy torts multiplied quickly. Today nearly every state recognizes torts based on the article, and there have been thousands of privacy tort cases.

To make change happen, ideas are just the starting point—they are not self-executing. In this case, it took the lawyer in *Roberson* dusting off Warren and Brandeis's theory from more than a decade before. It took people who discussed and criticized the case, enough to gain the attention of the New York legislature. It took legislators to pass the law. As more states created privacy torts via courts or legislatures, it took lawyers to bring the cases, judges to recognize the torts, and politicians to introduce bills.

Scholars contributed, too. William Prosser, the most famous torts scholar of his day, wrote about the Warren and Brandeis privacy torts in his treatise.[11] He subsequently published an important article about privacy torts, and he added them to the American Law Institute's *Restatement of Torts*, a highly influential document that judges look to for guidance.[12] The inclusion of the privacy torts in the Restatement convinced many judges to recognize them.

Ultimately, the story about the Warren and Brandeis torts took a rather disappointing turn. After achieving great success in the mid-20th century, the torts ossified. By mid-century, what had begun as an open-ended genesis of new torts to meet emerging technological challenges had turned into a rigid set of only four torts. Courts refused to adapt the elements of the existing torts to new situations, instead opting to parrot back the elements recorded in the *Restatement of Torts*.[13] Today, as a result, the privacy torts don't work well in situations involving the collection, use, and transfer of personal data in the digital age, and new torts aren't being generated. The privacy torts, which used to be central to the protection of privacy, are now of little relevance to society's most pressing privacy issues.

In the end, we can see that William Prosser perhaps had a version of the Midas touch. He turned the privacy torts into legal gold, leading to their legitimization in the law and vastly increasing their acceptance and adoption. But his touch seemed to freeze tort law in place, and in the years since it has failed to evolve to keep pace with technology.

If Warren and Brandeis were alive today, they would surely be disappointed by the current state of tort law. Brandeis believed in the importance of legal dynamism, expressed most eloquently when he declared as a Justice of the US Supreme Court that "our contemplation cannot be only of what has been, but of what may be."[14] For Brandeis, rigidity is a fatal flaw, especially in laws that must address rapidly changing technologies.

The argument of "The Right to Privacy" was that the law must evolve and adapt to address threats to privacy posed by new technologies. In other words, Warren and Brandeis were calling for legal innovation to respond to technological innovation.[15]

Looking back on the more than 130 years following the publication of the article, we initially see constricted thinking about privacy law, followed by a blossoming of creative thinking, then constriction and ossification, leading to a withering of the law and its waning effectiveness. A clear lesson emerges from this story: The law works best when forged by creative and flexible thinkers. Rigid and narrow thinking stultifies the law and renders it incapable of keeping pace with new technologies. For privacy law to be effective, courts and policymakers should recover the spirit of innovation that made Warren and Brandeis's article glow so bright.

Privacy Is Complicated, But the Law Is Too Simple

Privacy is immensely complicated, yet the law treats it too simplistically. I was drawn to the subject of privacy because of its complexity. I was a literature major in college, and also deeply immersed in philosophy, sociology, and history. As a humanities person to the core, I was particularly drawn to issues that were messy, nuanced, dynamic, and contextual. Of all the issues arising from the nascent internet, privacy seemed like a vast jungle, unexplored and untamed, and every issue it raised resembled a near-impenetrable tangle of vines. After twenty-five years exploring privacy issues, I'm still in the jungle. Though I now know enough not to get lost and even to make some headway, I still can't tame it.

As a law professor, I've focused on how the law reckons with privacy. I've studied how the law has evolved. And I've noticed that the law often has a flaw that prevents it from succeeding—it stubbornly resists privacy's complexity.

Of course, the law is generally required to simplify. Life is too varied and nuanced for the law to be able to address it in all its richness. Rules are generalities; if there were a new rule for each and every unique situation, we'd drown in an endless sea of rules.

But rules mustn't be too simple either. Rules can't be so divorced from the realities of life that they end up fitting many situations poorly. But far too often, privacy laws neglect key nuances and dimensions of privacy, a problem that occurs over and over again in many different ways.

Privacy law often attempts to address privacy in a binary manner— for example, by classifying things as either private or public, or by viewing consent as either all or nothing. But it is past time for the law to move beyond crude simplicity and recognize privacy's nuances.

Privacy isn't as black-and-white as the law often treats it. Privacy is a spectrum with many dimensions; nearly everything is gray. Privacy is often better protected when personal data doesn't flow so readily, when data remains obscure, when data is forgotten, and when data is fragmented and dispersed.

An example of an exemplary regulatory action involves a case in which the department store Sears offered users software that functioned as spyware. Users were naturally surprised to realize that they had unknowingly installed spyware onto their computers. Sears had actually disclosed in its privacy notice the fact that the software would spy, and such a disclosure is generally sufficient for organizations under US law. But the US Federal Trade Commission (FTC) concluded that the notice wasn't conspicuous enough, that for something as unexpected and invasive as spyware it wasn't sufficient to bury the information in a lengthy privacy notice that most people wouldn't read. The FTC deemed the privacy notice by Sears to be "unfair" and thus a violation of the FTC Act, which prohibits deceptive and unfair acts and practices.

The *Sears* case generated howls from many in industry who wanted to retain the existing clear rule that any practice would be okay if stated in a privacy notice. After *Sears*, the rule indeed became muddier: basically, *Notice must be appropriate for the circumstances.* Under the simplistic rule that industry wanted, organizations were able to unthinkingly check off notice on a checklist; the muddy rule, by contrast, would require a judgment call involving more thinking. Under the *Sears* rule, companies today are no longer totally safe when they disclose their practices, because a regulator might disagree with their judgment about what is appropriate. This creates uncertainty regarding the law, which companies never like.

In my view, the *Sears* case was a triumph. In it, the FTC recognized that privacy was not as simple as the mere existence of notice. Instead, the rule introduced a qualitative dimension requiring thinking and evaluation in place of a robotic checkbox response. Judgment must be used, and companies must always worry, *Is this enough?* But this worry seems to me to be a wonderful thing, like a stubborn grain of sand in an oyster that might produce a pearl.

Organizations often address privacy with the language of compliance. They readily digest regulatory requirements into their bureaucracies, developing mechanical and automated approaches that are inexpensive and easy and that reduce the issue of privacy to processes of compliance. They want clear, simple rules that provide absolute certainty and can be implemented without much thought or judgment. Compliance becomes a rote exercise.[16]

But the more appropriate language for privacy is the language of ethics, language that may be vaguer and far less concrete. Ethics require judgment and thought, which are key to the evolution of privacy. Privacy laws work best when they force organizations to engage in the deliberation of ethics and deny them the comfort of using only the formalities of compliance. Privacy laws should be messy and open-ended, dynamic and evolving; rather than being unambiguous, they should require challenging judgment calls.

Making Enforcement Meaningful

Law is not just a set of rules; it is an activity, an ongoing practice. There is no end—it is always developing. Rather than looking for the perfect recipe, we should instead be learning how to cook better.

Laws on the page often vary considerably from how they work in practice. Laws can falter if they are enforced without rigor, as in those countries that have enacted a comprehensive privacy law in the likeness of the GDPR yet have failed to enforce it. And many privacy laws fail to include meaningful enforcement provisions. Without effective enforcement, legal principles are like cardboard cutouts on a stage with nothing behind them. As a result, organizations will nod in agreement but do little to change their behavior.

If companies can avoid doing more than the bare minimum, then they often will. As I said earlier, organizations typically want to make things simple and efficient by devising routines and processes that can be done almost habitually. But safeguarding privacy requires constant thought and judgment, and effective enforcement requires that regulators ensure that organizations are engaging in this deeper analysis rather than superficial routines.

Privacy laws ultimately win or lose by their ground game. Strong enforcement can elevate a flawed law (though often only so much). Weak enforcement, however, can completely undermine even a strong law, effectively gutting its protections and thereby hollowing out its principles. Unfortunately, enforcement agencies are far too often underfunded, understaffed, and shackled by other limitations that limit their effectiveness.

The Virtues of a Case-by-Case Approach

The common law represents an ideal approach to addressing the dynamic realities of technological change. Under the common law, judges have leeway to adjust and develop the law, case by case, in order to address new challenges. The common law works by constraining judges to follow precedent, to base their decisions on prior decisions. New situations are addressed through analogical reasoning—that is, by noting similarities to previous situations.

Although the common law approach can be messy and uneven, it is also typically flexible and capable of evolving. Contrary to myths that the law is slow and lumbering, law professor Joshua Fairfield aptly describes law as "social technology" that can be nimble and dynamic.[17]

Even where statutes are concerned, a common-law approach may be useful. Statutes can be drafted in ways that leave room for evolving interpretation. For example, the US FTC Act broadly prohibits "unfair and deceptive" acts and practices. This law has been interpreted primarily by a federal agency—the FTC—through a series of enforcement actions. In the mid-1990s, more than fifty years after this provision was drafted, the FTC started using it as a way to protect privacy, and its language turned out to be expansive enough to encompass this new mission.[18]

In work with Woodrow Hartzog, I have characterized the FTC approach as a common law-style approach.[19] When executed well, the common law approach deftly navigates between flexibility and rigor. Respect for precedent helps maintain consistency, and case decisions over time generate specificity and a more concrete set of rules. The common law approach can work with many types of law, including constitutional and statutory law, as long as the language at issue is sufficiently open.

Of course, the common law approach is likely to fail when executed poorly. Disrespect for precedent, poorly reasoned cases, inconsistent decisions, and other problems can doom attempts to base cases on the common law. It is hard for any approach or system to work well when corrupted by people with poor judgment. Though we always hope that our institutions will save us, institutions will falter when run by people bent on mischief, intoxicated with their own ideologies, or careless or indifferent.

A law that is broad and flexible can be counterproductive unless enforcement is vigorous and creative. Law isn't self-executing; it depends not only upon good judgment and sound reasoning but upon being interpreted and enforced in good faith.

The Virtues of a Polycentric Approach

I often hear from commentators a strong desire for a unified approach to privacy—a single federal agency to focus exclusively on privacy. But I am not sure that such an approach is ideal; instead, a more polycentric approach might be more effective and durable.[20] Polycentric governance involves a multitude of different actors and mechanisms, avoiding the problems that can beset unified governance systems, such as when enforcement agencies are captured or weakened by political actors. A polycentric approach also allows for greater experimentation and varying approaches.

To regulate an issue as sprawling and complicated as privacy, we need different regulatory agencies, individual lawsuits, and industry codes, as well as many different laws. The United States has long been criticized for lacking a comprehensive federal privacy law, and rightly so. But many bills that have been proposed have provisions that preempt other laws, which is bad for the future of privacy regulation. The overall development of the law benefits from a multitude of approaches. What would work best is a federal comprehensive law providing the baseline of data protection. Other laws could provide stricter protection rather than being blocked by a single one-size-fits-all law.

The Humanities Are Essential

The challenge of appropriately addressing the problems of privacy and technology can't be met without a solid grounding in the humanities. Privacy is contextual and nuanced, and it is not something that can be readily automated or reduced to simplistic processes or checklists.

In our zeal to embrace technology, it is easy to lose sight of the humanities, which, with their moral complexity, may seem like an arduous detour through foggy terrain. But although the humanities don't provide easy answers, they are essential to grappling with the difficult ethical issues that technology creates.

The humanities teach the ability to see things from different perspectives, to develop a richer understanding of what other people are feeling and experiencing. The humanities enable us to be more creative, to think in new ways, to appreciate nuances, and to develop a richer understanding of human behavior. To address the problems technology poses for privacy, policymakers can't think like mechanics, but must instead draw on their wisdom, judgment, and creativity. For the creative policymaker steeped in the humanities, the range of options becomes much broader and the usable tools become much more numerous.

A Bolder Path for Law

When considering the challenges new technologies are posing for privacy, many people are quite pessimistic about the possibility of regulating. Technology appears to move too fast for the law to keep up. At the beginning of this book, I asked: *Are we doomed?* Many people seem to be resigned to a nightmarish future without privacy. But this defeatism serves the interests of the organizations that want to be regulated weakly or not at all. They want us to become overwhelmed by technology's complexity, speed, might, and majesty so that we accept the futility of regulating technology with anything but a light touch.

But we need not give in to defeatism, and we can do something, though it is a different path from the one most laws are taking. Currently, most privacy laws—even the best of them such as the GDPR—don't seem to lead to significant changes in how organizations do business. Laws impose documentation and compliance requirements that produce modest cost and headaches for organizations, but these requirements only occasionally move the needle in a significant way. A majority of privacy laws offer people various privacy rights that are impossible to use at scale and that most people ultimately don't use.

After discussing with me the terrifying threats to privacy by new technologies, countless interviewers ask me what individuals can do to protect their privacy. They want to end on a positive note and give people a sense of hope and empowerment. But I hate this question. I could rattle off a few small things people can do—such as read privacy notices, opt out of certain data uses, avoid putting too much personal data online, access their records and request the deletion of their data—but these things are futile. They create the illusion that individuals can meaningfully protect themselves if they just work hard enough. Instead, I prefer to tell people the truth. No matter

how hard they try, they can't even come close to protecting themselves. The best thing people can do is to demand that policymakers
do something meaningful. People shouldn't accept the anemic laws
they're being given. Policymakers are continually enacting privacy
laws with approaches that are long known to be ineffective. Instead of
serving people a hearty nutritious meal, policymakers are giving them
the same old broth with a dash of spice to pass it off as something new.
The best thing people can do to protect their privacy is to insist that
these laws be sent back to the kitchen and to demand laws that require
rigorous accountability.

For the law to protect privacy effectively, it must move past the stul-
tifying myths about technology that have stood in the way. The *Myth of
the Privacy Paradox* impedes the genesis of law by falsely claiming that
people don't really care about privacy. The *Myth of Technology Exceptionalism* wrongly attempts to put technology beyond longstanding
legal rules and principles. The *Myth that Regulation Stifles Innovation*
is often just a false attempt at scaremongering; it is really just a ploy
to allow the creators and users of technology to avoid accountability.
The *Myth that Changes in Degree Don't Matter* deters regulation by
overplaying the difficulty of drawing lines. The *Myth that the Law is
an Interloper* falsely views technology as a naturally-occurring phenomenon independent of law when technology is actually already
shaped by law. The *Myth of Technology Neutrality* fosters a false vision
of technology as pure and objective when, in fact, technology is deeply
human and is infected by human bias and flaws. All of these myths fuel
the reluctance to regulate to address the challenges technology poses
to privacy. These myths constantly jump in the way to deter or weaken
the law from demanding that creators and users of technology be held
responsible for the harms they cause.

The law already plays a major negative role in the way technology is changing privacy. Law facilitates information flow. It bathes
companies in immunities and exemptions from liability for the harms
created by their technologies, sheltering them from accountability for
the consequences and social costs. By deferring too much to technological design and shielding companies from the consequences of
their activity, the law creates architectures of vulnerability, facilitating the collection and use of personal information on a vast scale

and allowing potentially harmful uses of this information without adequate safeguards.

Power has been a major theme in this book. Privacy is about power. Digital technologies increase information and knowledge about people, enabling personal data to flow more readily, to tether people to a permanent record and prevent them from growth and reinvention, to erode practical obscurity, to aggregate pieces of data into massive dossiers about people, and to make inferences that reveal facets about their lives they don't expect to reveal. These technologies transform the nature of judgment and decisions; they enable predictions about people that defy human agency, facilitate automated decisions that omit people's uniqueness as persons, place people's reputations in peril, and present the illusion of consent, bestowing false legitimacy and unwarranted power on the entities implementing the technologies. Digital technologies also shape thought and behavior, thwarting people's expectations of privacy, sculpting people's choices though design, manipulating people's behavior, influencing people's perception and emotional responses through controlling distance, and establishing relationships not of trust but of unequal power. These technologies affect power by shifting it from individuals to mighty organizations or by giving power to individuals who use it to attack each other. Technologies facilitate control over individuals through surveillance, increase inequality, and enable systematic identification. They enhance power by lowering the costs of collecting, using, and transferring data and enabling enormous scaling.

Only by focusing on power can the law best address the problems of privacy and technology. Only by establishing the right legal structure and the right incentives can the law succeed in holding creators and users of technology accountable. Instead, the law often does the opposite. It empowers the powerful; it makes exceptions for new technologies from traditional mechanisms of accountability; it allows organizations to construct business models based on massive scale and cheap expenses that are only possible by externalizing costs to individuals. Courts often fail to recognize privacy harms or trivialize them. Even when there are clear violations of privacy laws, courts use creativity not to help victims but to close off ways to obtain redress. Through its actions, the law is sending a message regarding new technologies:

to create and use them irresponsibly and to care mainly about growth and profit. When harm is caused, the law often finds a way to help the wrongdoer evade responsibility.

To avoid a dystopian future, we must demand that the law take a different path. We must dispel all the myths that prevent regulatory progress. We need laws that stop putting the onus on ill-equipped individuals to protect their own privacy and that start holding organizations accountable for the consequences they cause. We must insist that policymakers abandon antiquated and simplistic notions of privacy and address privacy in its full nuance and complexity. The law must move beyond rote and hollow compliance exercises and toward a deeper approach rooted in ethical judgment. The law must be unwavering in core ethical principles such as accountability but flexible and nuanced in how to implement these principles in practice.

It all begins with how we see and understand privacy and technology. Privacy must no longer be trivialized or viewed as solely an individual preference. Privacy is an essential social value, and it undergirds many other key social values such as freedom and democracy. We must question the framing and metaphors that shape our conception of digital technologies. We must look beyond what appears to be neutral, and we must see the oft-concealed human elements within technology. We must recognize that technology is always created with power and for power; it is a tool created by humans and wielded by humans for human aims. We can't be reticent about regulating technological design, for it is an exercise of power with dramatic implications for privacy.

Ultimately, a major impediment to protecting privacy against the challenges posed by new technologies is to view it as about regulating technology. This conjures up all the myths, frames, and metaphors that make the task seem so daunting, if not impossible. But what really must be regulated is not technology but humans—either individual people or organizations, which are essentially groups of people who are bestowed special privileges by the law. The bottom line is that we must regulate the humans who create and use these technologies and hold them accountable for the harms they cause. But far too often, when new technologies are involved, policymakers' vision becomes clouded, and the law veers from the well-trodden path that has yielded success for centuries—holding actors responsible for the consequences of their actions.

I began this book by discussing the frequent declarations of the death of privacy. Privacy isn't yet dead . . . but it isn't secure. We can't escape from the worry that privacy may be dying, nor should we. As technology evolves, privacy will always be in danger. We must constantly work to keep it alive, like emergency room doctors desperately trying to save a critical patient. We can never rest. Protecting privacy is destined to be an ongoing project, not a problem to be solved.

Many of the challenges technology poses for privacy weren't created by technology—these problems already existed. But technology exacerbates and amplifies; it speeds things up and makes things bigger. We must address the threats it now presents and we must keep at it, without allowing either fear or worship of technology to get in the way.

Acknowledgments

Countless individuals have helped me forge my views on privacy through their insightful scholarship, their illuminating conversations, or both. Here I list a few of the many to whom I owe my gratitude: Alessandro Acquisti, Ifeoma Ajunwa, Anita Allen, Josef Ansorge, Jack Balkin, Solon Barocas, Elettra Bietti, Hannah Bloch-Wehba, danah boyd, Dan Burk, Ryan Calo, Anupam Chander, Danielle Citron, Julie Cohen, Ella Corren, Lorrie Cranor, Kate Crawford, Deven Desai, Mary Anne Franks, Oscar Gandy, Robert Gellman, James Grimmelmann, Woodrow Hartzog, Mireille Hildebrandt, David Hoffman, Marcia Hofmann, Chris Hoofnagle, Aziz Huq, Elizabeth Joh, Margot Kaminski, Ian Kerr, Orin Kerr, Pauline Kim, Raymond Ku, Lawrence Lessig, Karen Levy, Tiffani Li, Florencia Marotta-Wurgler, Yuki Matsumi, Andrea Matwyshyn, Bill McGeveran, Deirdre Mulligan, Helen Nissenbaum, Martha Nussbaum, Paul Ohm, Frank Pasquale, Jari Peters, Robert Post, Priscilla Regan, Joel Reidenberg, Neil Richards, Jeff Rosen, Pamela Samuelson, Bruce Schneier, Lauren Scholz, Paul Schwartz, Andrew Selbst, Spiros Simitis, Chris Slobogin, Alicia Solow-Niederman, Lior Strahilevitz, William Stuntz, Michael Sullivan, Peter Swire, Omer Tene, Charlotte Tschider, Sandra Wachter, Ari Waldman, Kate Weisburd, Alan Westin, Chris Wolf, Tal Zarsky, Elana Zeide, and Jonathan Zittrain.

For extremely helpful comments on the manuscript itself, I want to thank Chris Hoofnagle, Susan Schulman, Ari Waldman, and Ryan Calo.

About the Author

Daniel J. Solove is the Eugene L. and Barbara A. Bernard Professor of Intellectual Property and Technology Law at the George Washington University Law School. One of the world's leading experts in privacy law, Solove is the author of more than 10 books and 100 articles about privacy. He has also written a children's fiction book about privacy. He is one of the most cited law professors in the law and technology field.

Professor Solove has been interviewed and quoted in hundreds of media articles and broadcasts and has been a consultant for many Fortune 500 companies and celebrities. He has more than 1 million LinkedIn followers. His work is available at www.danielsolove.com.

Notes

Prelims

1. Michael Sullivan & Daniel J. Solove, Can Pragmatism Be Radical?: Richard Posner and Legal Pragmatism, 113 *Yale L. J.* 687 (2003); Michael Sullivan & Daniel J. Solove, Radical Pragmatism, in *The Cambridge Companion to Pragmatism* (Alan Malacowski ed., 2013).

Part 1

1. Ari Ezra Waldman, *Industry Unbound: The Inside Story of Privacy, Data, and Corporate Power* (2021); Waldman, Designing Without Privacy, 55 *Hous. L. Rev.* 659 (2018).
2. Shoshana Zuboff, *The Age of Surveillance Capitalism: The Fight for a Human Future at the New Frontier of Power* 11 (2019).

What is Privacy?

1. Ludwig Wittgenstein, *Philosophical Investigations* § 65. Translated by G.E.M. Anscombe.
2. Daniel J. Solove, *Understanding Privacy* (2008).
3. *Id.*

What is Technology?

1. Zia Haider Rahman, *In the Light of What We Know* 134 (2015).
2. Orly Lobel, *The Equality Machine: Harnessing Digital Technology for a Brighter, More Inclusive Future* (2022).

Why Is Privacy Important?

1. On the importance of privacy, I strongly recommend Neil Richards's eloquent and compelling book *Why Privacy Matters* (2021).
2. *See, e.g.,* Ellen Alderman & Caroline Kennedy, *The Right to Privacy* xv (1995) ("[P]rivacy is, by definition, a personal right."); Restatement (Second) of Torts § 652(I) comment (a) ("The right protected by the action for invasion of privacy is a personal right, peculiar to the individual whose privacy is invaded").
3. Priscilla M. Regan, *Legislating Privacy: Technology, Social Values, and Public Policy* (1995).
4. John Dewey, Ethics, *in* 5 *Middle Works* 268 (Jo Ann Boydston ed., 1978), (1908).
5. *See* Julie E. Cohen, Examined Lives: Information Privacy and the Subject as Object, 52 *Stan. L. Rev.* 1373 (2000); Paul M. Schwartz, Privacy and Democracy in Cyberspace, 52 *Vand. L. Rev.* 1607 (1999); Robert C. Post, The Social Foundations of Privacy: Community and Self in the Common Law Tort, 77 *Cal. L. Rev.* 957 (1989).
6. Daniel J. Solove, *Nothing to Hide: The False Tradeoff Between Privacy and Security* (2011); Daniel J. Solove, "I've Got Nothing to Hide" and Other Misunderstandings of Privacy, 44 *San Diego L. Rev.* 745 (2007).
7. Bruce Schneier, *Beyond Fear: Thinking Sensibly About Security in an Uncertain World* 38–39 (2003).

8. Daniel J. Solove & Neil M. Richards, Privacy's Other Path: Recovering the Law of Confidentiality, 96 *Geo. L. J.* 123 (2007); Neil Richards & Woodrow Hartzog, Privacy's Trust Gap: A Review, 126 *Yale L. J.* 908 (2017); Ari Ezra Waldman, *Privacy as Trust: Information Privacy for an Information Age* (2018).
9. Neil Richards, *Intellectual Privacy: Rethinking Civil Liberties in the Digital Age* (2015).
10. Danielle Keats Citron, Sexual Privacy, 128 *Yale L. J.* 1870, 1874 (2019).

Framing and Metaphors

1. Woodrow Hartzog, The Fight to Frame Privacy, 111 *Mich. L. Rev.* 1021 (2013).
2. Ryan Calo, Robots as Legal Metaphors, 30 *Harv. J. L. & Tech.* 209, 211 (2016).
3. Leo Katz discovered this gem. Leo Katz, *Bad Acts and Guilty Minds: Conundrums of the Criminal Law* 197 (1987).
4. Alessandro Acquisti, Leslie K. John & George Loewenstein, What Is Privacy Worth?, 42 *J. Leg. Studies* 249 (2013).
5. Woodrow Hartzog, *Privacy's Blueprint: The Battle to Control the Design of New Technologies* (2018).
6. Steven Johnson, *Interface Culture: How New Technology Transforms the Way We Create & Communicate* (1997).
7. Ifeoma Ajunwa, The Paradox of Automation as Anti-Bias Intervention, 41 *Cardozo L. Rev.* 1671, 1704–07 (2020).
8. Kate Crawford, *Atlas of AI: Power, Politics, and the Planetary Costs of Artificial Intelligence* (2021); Rebecca Crootof, Margot E. Kaminski & W. Nicholson Price II, Humans in the Loop, 76 *Vand. L. Rev.* 429 (2023).
9. Margot E. Kaminski, Binary Governance: Lessons from the GDPR's Approach to Algorithmic Accountability, 92 *S. Cal. L. Rev.* 1529, 1538–39 (2019).
10. John Dewey, *Logic: The Theory of Inquiry* 112 (Jo Ann Boydston ed., 1991) (1938).
11. Daniel J. Solove, *The Digital Person: Technology and Privacy in the Information Age* (2004).
12. *Id.*
13. Smitha Milli, Micah Carroll, Sashrika Pandey, Yike Wang & Anca D. Dragan, Twitter's Algorithm: Amplifying Anger, Animosity, and Affective Polarization, arXiv.org, https://www.researchgate.net/publication/371124077_Twitter's_Algorithm_Amplifying_Anger_Animosity_and_Affective_Polarization (May 26, 2023).
14. Danielle Keats Citron, *The Fight for Privacy: Protecting Dignity, Identity, and Love in the Digital Age* (2022); Mary Anne Franks, "Revenge Porn" Reform: A View from the Front Lines, 69 *Fla. L. Rev.* 1251 (2017).
15. William Brady, Social Media Algorithms Warp How People Learn from Each Other, Research Shows (Aug. 21, 2023), The Conversation, https://theconversation.com/social-media-algorithms-warp-how-people-learn-from-each-other-research-shows-211172

Myths

1. Daniel J. Solove, The Myth of the Privacy Paradox, 89 *Geo. Wash. L. Rev.* 1 (2021).
2. Daniel J. Solove & Woodrow Hartzog, *Breached! Why Data Security Law Fails and How to Improve It* 106-09 (2022).
3. Jack M. Balkin, Digital Speech and Democratic Culture: A Theory of Freedom of Expression for the Information Society, 79 *N.Y.U. L. Rev.* 1 (2004).
4. As Margot Kaminski aptly observes, law and technology "are not just one-way forces but dynamic, dialectical relationships." Margot Kaminski, Technological 'Disruption' of the Law's Imagined Scene: Some Lessons from Lex Informatica, 36 *Berkeley Tech. L. J.* 883 (2021).

5. Amy Kapczynski, The Law of Informational Capitalism, 129 *Yale L. J.* 5, 1460 (2020).
6. With Yuki Matsumi, I explore several related faulty arguments about AI, including the argument that AI can make decisions better and more neutrally than humans. *See* Daniel J. Solove & Hideyuki Matsumi, AI, Algorithms, and Awful Humans, 92 *Fordham L. Rev.* 1923 (2024).
7. Kate Crawford, *Atlas of AI: Power, Politics, and the Planetary Costs of Artificial Intelligence* (2021); Margot E. Kaminski, Binary Governance: Lessons from the GDPR's Approach to Algorithmic Accountability, 92 *S. Cal. L. Rev.* 1529 (2019).
8. Sandra G. Mayson, Bias In, Bias Out, 128 *Yale L. J.* 2218 (2019).
9. Kate Crawford, *Artificial Intelligence's White Guy Problem*, N.Y. Times (June 25, 2016).
10. Jerry Z. Muller, *The Tyranny of Metrics* 40 (2018).
11. Darrell Huff, *How to Lie with Statistics* (1954).

Part 2

Information and Knowledge

1. Samuel D. Warren & Louis D. Brandeis, The Right to Privacy, 4 *Har. Law Rev.* 193 (1890).
2. Daniel J. Solove, *The Digital Person: Technology and Privacy in the Information Age* (2004).
3. Lior Jacob Strahilevitz, A Social Networks Theory of Privacy, 72 *U. Chi. L. Rev.* 919 (2005).
4. Some notable exceptions where laws protect data even when it flows to other entities are the GDPR and the Health Information Portability and Accountability Act (HIPAA).
5. Helen Nissenbaum, *Privacy in Context: Technology, Policy, and the Integrity of Social Life* (2009); Daniel J. Solove, Conceptualizing Privacy, 90 *Cal. L. Rev.* 1087 (2002).
6. Meg Leta Jones, *Ctrl + Z: The Right to Be Forgotten* (2016).
7. Viktor Mayer-Schönberger, *Delete: The Virtue of Forgetting in the Digital Age* (2009).
8. John Dewey, *Experience and Nature* 167 (Jo Ann Boydston ed., 1987) (1925).
9. Erving Goffman, *The Presentation of Self in Everyday Life* (1959).
10. Daniel J. Solove, The Limitations of Privacy Rights, 98 *Notre Dame L. Rev.* 975 (2023).
11. Woodrow Hartzog & Frederic Stutzman, The Case for Online Obscurity, 101 *Cal. L. Rev.* 1 (2013).
12. Kashmir Hill, *Your Face Belongs to Us: A Secretive Startup's Quest to End Privacy as We Know It* (2023).
13. Daniel J. Solove, Access and Aggregation: Privacy, Public Records, and the Constitution, 86 *Minn. L. Rev.* 1137, 1176–78 (2002).
14. Department of Justice v. Reporters Committee for Freedom of the Press, 489 U.S. 749 (1989).
15. Solove, The Digital Person, *supra*.
16. Carpenter v. United States, 138 S. Ct. 2206 (2018).
17. Hideyuki Matsumi, Predictions and Privacy: Should There Be Rules About Using Personal Data to Forecast the Future?, 48 *Cumb. L. Rev.* 149 (2018); Alicia Solow-Niederman, Information Privacy and the Inference Economy, 117 *Nw. U. L. Rev.* 357 (2022).
18. Charles Duhigg, *How Companies Learn Your Secrets*, N.Y. Times Magazine (Feb. 16, 2012).

19. Charles Duhigg, *The Power of Habit: Why We Do What We Do in Life and Business* 182–97, 209–10 (2012).
20. Oscar H. Gandy, Jr., *Coming to Terms with Chance: Engaging Rational Discrimination and Cumulative Disadvantage* 63 (2009); Jessica M. Eaglin, Constructing Recidivism Risk, 67 *Emory L. J.* 59, 72 (2017); Sandra G. Mayson, Bias In, Bias Out, 128 *Yale L. J.* 2218, 2224 (2019).
21. Jeffrey Dastin, *Amazon Scraps Secret AI Recruiting Tool That Showed Bias Against Women*, Reuters (Oct. 10, 2018).
22. Ifeoma Ajunwa, The Paradox of Automation as Anti-Bias Intervention, 41 *Cardozo L. Rev.* 1671, 1681 (2020); Solon Barocas & Andrew D. Selbst, Big Data's Disparate Impact, 104 *Cal. L. Rev.* 671 (2016); Anupam Chander, The Racist Algorithm?, 115 *Mich. L. Rev.* 1023, 1036 (2017).
23. Sandra Wachter & Brent Mittelstadt, A Right to Reasonable Inferences: Re-Thinking Data Protection Law in the Age of Big Data and AI, 2019 *Colum. Bus. L. Rev.* 494 (2019).

Judgments and Decisions

1. Hideyuki Matsumi, Predictions and Privacy: Should There Be Rules About Using Personal Data to Forecast the Future?, 48 *Cumb. L. Rev.* 149 (2018).
2. Andrew Guthrie Ferguson, *The Rise of Big Data Policing: Surveillance, Race, and the Future of Law Enforcement* (2017).
3. Hideyuki Matsumi & Daniel J. Solove, The Prediction Society: AI and the Problems of Forecasting the Future (2023), forthcoming, 2025 *U. Illinois L. Rev.* __ (2025), https://ssrn.com/abstract=4453869.
4. Carissa Véliz, If AI Is Predicting Your Future, Are You Still Free? Wired (Dec. 27, 2021).
5. Quote Investigator, *We Cannot Predict the Future, But We Can Invent It* (2012), https://quoteinvestigator.com/2012/09/27/invent-the-future/.
6. Matsumi & Solove, The Prediction Society, *supra*.
7. Sandra G. Mayson, Bias In, Bias Out, 128 *Yale L. J.* 2218, 2224 (2019); Anupam Chander, The Racist Algorithm?, 115 *Mich. L. Rev.* 1023, 1036 (2017); Pauline T. Kim, Manipulating Opportunity, 106 *Va. L. Rev.* 867, 870 (2020).
8. Cary Coglianese & Lavi M. Ben Dor, AI in Adjudication and Administration, 86 *Brook. L. Rev.* 791 (2021); Cass R. Sunstein, Governing by Algorithm? No Noise and (Potentially) Less Bias, 71 *Duke L. J.* 1175 (2022).
9. Oscar H. Gandy, Jr., Coming to Terms with Chance: Engaging Rational Discrimination and Cumulative Disadvantage 63 (2009).
10. Katrina Geddes, The Death of the Legal Subject, 25 *Vand. J. Ent. & Tech. L.* 1, 5 (2023).
11. Nassim Nicholas Taleb, *The Black Swan: The Impact of the Highly Improbable* xvii, 149, 138, 149 (2007).
12. Cathy O'Neil, *Weapons of Math Destruction: How Big Data Increases Inequality and Threatens Democracy* (2016).
13. Hideyuki Matsumi, The Failure of the Right to Rectification, draft on file with author.
14. Wisconsin v. Loomis, 881 N. W. 2d 749 (Wis. 2016).
15. Ben Green, The Flaws of Policies Requiring Human Oversight of Government Algorithms, 45 *Comput. Law Secur. Rev.* 1, 7 (2022).
16. For a critique of the use of trade secrets in this context, see Rebecca Wexler, Life, Liberty, and Trade Secrets: Intellectual Property in the Criminal Justice System, 70 *Stan. L. Rev.* 1343 (2018).

17. Jeff Larson, Surya Mattu, Lauren Kirchner & Julia Angwin, How We Analyzed the COMPAS Recidivism Algorithm, at 1 (2016), https://www.propublica.org/article/how-we-analyzed-the-compas-recidivism-algorithm.

18. Daniel J. Solove & Hideyuki Matsumi, AI, Algorithms, and Awful Humans, 92 *Fordham L. Rev.* 1923 (2024).

19. Daniel J. Solove, *The Digital Person: Technology and Privacy in the Information Age* 49 (2004); Dan L. Burk, Algorithmic Legal Metrics, 96 *Notre Dame L. Rev.* 1147, 1158 (2021).

20. Quoted in Chris Wiggins and Matthew L. Jones, *How Data Happened: A History from the Age of Reason to the Age of Algorithms* 26 (2023).

21. Dan L. Burk, Algorithmic Legal Metrics, 96 *Notre Dame L. Rev.* 1147 (2021).

22. Jerry Z. Muller, *The Tyranny of Metrics* 18 (2018) (quoting William Bruce Cameron, *Informal Sociology: A Casual Introduction to Sociological Thinking* (1963)).

23. W. H. Auden, The Unknown Citizen [1940], in W. H. Auden: *Collected Shorter Poems 1927–1957* (Edward Mendelson ed., 1976).

24. GDPR art. 25.

25. Rebecca Crootof, Margot E. Kaminski & W. Nicholson Price II, Humans in the Loop, 76 *Vand. L. Rev.* 429, 437 (2023).

26. Green, *supra*, 12.

27. Daniel J. Solove, *The Future of Reputation: Gossip, Rumor, and Privacy on the Internet* (2007).

28. Danielle Keats Citron, *Hate Crimes in Cyberspace* (2014).

29. Danielle K. Citron & Robert Chesney, Deep Fakes: A Looming Challenge for Privacy, Democracy, and National Security, 107 *Cal. L. Rev.* 1753 (2019).

30. Niraj Chokshi, "That Wasn't Mark Twain: How a Misquotation Is Born," N.Y. Times (Apr. 26, 2017), https://www.nytimes.com/2017/04/26/books/famous-misquotations.html.

31. Eugene Volokh, The Law of Pseudonymous Litigation, 73 *Hastings L. J.* 1353 (2022).

32. Solove, *Future of Reputation, supra.*

33. Daniel J. Solove, The Virtues of Knowing Less: Justifying Privacy Protections Against Disclosure, 53 *Duke L. J.* 967 (2003).

34. 47 U.S.C. § 230.

35. Danielle Keats Citron & Frank Pasquale, The Scored Society: Due Process for Automated Predictions, 89 *Wash. L. Rev.* 1 (2014).

36. Daniel J. Solove, Murky Consent: An Approach to the Fictions of Consent in Privacy Law, 104 *B. U. L. Rev.* 593 (2024).

37. Heidi M. Hurd, *The Moral Magic of Consent*, 2 Legal Theory 121, 123 (1996).

38. Elettra Bietti, Consent as a Free Pass: Platform Power and the Limits of the Informational Turn, 40 *Pace L. Rev.* 310, 313 (2020).

39. Neil Richards & Woodrow Hartzog, The Pathologies of Digital Consent, 96 *Wash. U. L. Rev.* 1461, 1463 (2019); Richard Warner & Robert Sloan, Beyond Notice and Choice: Privacy, Norms, and Consent, 14 *J. High Tech. L.* 370 (2013).

40. Daniel J. Solove, Privacy Self-Management and the Consent Dilemma, 126 *Harv. L. Rev.* 1880 (2013); Omri Ben-Shahar & Carl E. Schneider, *More Than You Wanted to Know: The Failure of Mandated Disclosure* (2014).

41. GDPR art. 4(11) (consent must be "freely given, specific, informed and unambiguous").

42. Ella Corren, The Consent Burden in Consumer and Digital Markets, 36 *Harv. J. L. & Tech.* 551 (2023).

43. Florencia Marotta-Wurgler, Will Increased Disclosure Help? Evaluating the Recommendations of the ALI's "Principles of the Law of Software Contracts," 78 *U. Chi. L. Rev.* 165, 182 (2011).

44. Nancy S. Kim, *Consentability: Consent and Its Limits* 81 (2019).

45. Solove, Murky Consent, *supra.*

Thought and Behavior

1. Smith v. Chase Manhattan Bank, 293 A.D.2d 598, 599 (N.Y. App. Div. 2002). In some cases, plaintiffs have fared better, but courts are very inconsistent in recognizing harm. *See* Danielle Keats Citron & Daniel J. Solove, Privacy Harms, 102 *B. U. L. Rev.* 793 (2022).

2. Joseph Turow, Jennifer King, Chris Jay Hoofnagle, Amy Bleakley & Michael Hennessy, Americans Reject Tailored Advertising and Three Activities That Enable It (September 29, 2009), SSRN, http://ssrn.com/abstract=1478214.

3. Daniel J. Solove & Woodrow Hartzog, The FTC and the New Common Law of Privacy, 114 *Colum. L. Rev.* 583 (2014).

4. Michelle Madejski, Maritza Johnson & Steven M. Bellovin, A Study of Privacy Settings Errors in an Online Social Network, DOI:10.1109/PerComW.2012.6197507 (2012).

5. Katz v. United States, 389 U.S. 347 (1967) (Harlan, J., concurring).

6. Smith v. Maryland, 442 U.S. 735 (1979) (no expectation of privacy in phone records); United States v. Miller, 425 U.S. 435 (1976) (no expectation of privacy in bank records).

7. California v. Greenwood, 486 U.S. 35 (1988) (no reasonable expectation in trash one discards, even if in opaque plastic bags).

8. Elizabeth E. Joh, Reclaiming "Abandoned" DNA: The Fourth Amendment and Genetic Privacy, 100 *Nw. U. L. Rev.* 857 (2006).

9. Florida v. Riley, 488 U.S. 445 (1989) (no expectation of privacy in one's property viewed overhead by police flying in a helicopter); Dow Chemical Co. v. United States, 476 U.S. 227 (1986) (no expectation of privacy in use of high-tech mapping camera).

10. Daniel J. Solove, *Nothing to Hide: The False Tradeoff Between Privacy and Security* (2011); Daniel J. Solove, Digital Dossiers and the Dissipation of Fourth Amendment Privacy, 75 *S. Cal. L. Rev.* 1083 (2002).

11. Daniel J. Solove, Fourth Amendment Pragmatism, 51 *B. C. L. Rev.* 1511 (2010).

12. Daniel J. Solove, *Understanding Privacy* (2008).

13. Joel Reidenberg, *Lex Informatica*: The Formulation of Information Policy Rules through Technology, 76 *Tex. L. Rev.* 553 (1997).

14. Steven Johnson, *Interface Culture: How New Technology Transforms the Way We Create and Communicate* 14, 19 (1997).

15. Woodrow Hartzog, *Privacy's Blueprint: The Battle to Control the Design of New Technologies* 23 (2018).

16. GDPR art. 25. The term "Privacy by Design" (abbreviated PbD) was coined by Ann Cavoukian, the former Information and Privacy Commissioner of Ontario, Canada.

17. Ari Ezra Waldman, Designing Without Privacy, 55 *Hous. L. Rev.* 659, 681–85 (2018).

18. Hartzog, Privacy's Blueprint, *supra*.

19. *See* José Ortega y Gasset, The Dehumanization of Art, in *A Modern Book of Esthetics* (Melvin Rader ed., 1952), 433–35 (1925).

20. Robert M. Cover, Violence and the Word, 95 *Yale L. J.* 1601, 1601 (1986).

21. Daniel Susser, Beate Roessler & Helen Nissenbaum, Online Manipulation: Hidden Influences in a Digital World, 4 *Geo. L. Tech. Rev.* 1 (2019); Cass R. Sunstein, Fifty Shades of Manipulation, 1 *J. Marketing Behav.* 213 (2015); Ryan Calo, Digital Market Manipulation, 82 *Geo. Wash. L. Rev.* 995 (2014); Shaun B. Spencer, The Problem of Online Manipulation, 2020 *U. Ill. L. Rev.* 959 (2020).

22. Daniel Kahneman, *Thinking, Fast and Slow* (2011).

23. Harry Brignull, Dark Patterns: Dirty Tricks Designers Use to Make People Do Stuff, 90 Percent of Everything (July 8, 2010).

24. California Consumer Privacy Act, Cal. Civ. Code § 1798.140; Colorado Privacy Act 6-1-1303.

25. Lopez v. United States, 373 U.S. 427 (1963); Hoffa v. United States, 385 U.S. 293 (1966); On Lee v. United States, 343 U.S. 747 (1952).
26. John M. Broder, Monica Lewinsky's Mother Fails in Bid to End Testimony, Wash. Post (Mar. 26, 1998).
27. Nader v. General Motors Corp., 255 N.E. 2d 765 (N.Y. Ct. App. 1970).
28. Daniel J. Solove & Neil M. Richards, Privacy's Other Path: Recovering the Law of Confidentiality, 96 Geo. L. J. 123 (2007).
29. Id.
30. Solove, *The Digital Person, supra*, at 102. This idea has been further developed in a number of articles, such as Jack M. Balkin, Information Fiduciaries and the First Amendment, 49 *U. C. Davis L. Rev.* 1183, 1186 (2016); Lauren Henry Scholz, Fiduciary Boilerplate: Locating Fiduciary Relationships in Information Age Consumer Transactions, 46 *J. Corp. L.* 143 (2020); Neil M. Richards & Woodrow Hartzog, A Duty of Loyalty for Privacy Law, 99 *Wash. U. L. Rev.* 961 (2021).
31. Richards & Hartzog, Duty of Loyalty, *supra.*

Power

1. John Perry Barlow, *A Declaration of the Independence of Cyberspace* (Feb. 8, 1996).
2. Lawrence Lessig, *Code and Other Laws of Cyberspace* (1999).
3. Michel Foucault, *Discipline and Punish: The Birth of the Prison* (Alan Sheridan trans., 2d ed. 1995) (1977). For an early work pointing out the panoptic effects of the burgeoning digital economy, see Oscar H. Gandy, Jr., *The Panoptic Sort: A Political Economy of Personal Information* (1993).
4. Julie E. Cohen, Examined Lives: Informational Privacy and the Subject as Object, 52 *Stan. L. Rev.* 1373 (2000). Paul M. Schwartz, Privacy and Democracy in Cyberspace, 52 Vand. L. Rev. 1607 (1999); Neil Richards, *Why Privacy Matters* (2021).
5. David Brin, *The Transparent Society: Will Technology Force Us to Choose Between Privacy and Freedom?* (1998).
6. John Gilliom, *Overseers of the Poor: Surveillance, Resistance, and the Limits of Privacy* (2001); Khiara M. Bridges, *The Poverty of Privacy Rights* (2017).
7. Alvaro M. Bedoya, Privacy as Civil Right, 50 *N. M. L. Rev.* 301 (2020); Mary Anne Franks, Democratic Surveillance, 30 *Harv. J. Law & Tech.* 425 (2017); Andrew Guthrie Ferguson, *The Rise of Big Data Policing: Surveillance, Race, and the Future of Law Enforcement* (2017).
8. Danielle Keats Citron, *Hate Crimes in Cyberspace* (2014); Danielle Keats Citron, Sexual Privacy, 128 *Yale L. J.* 1870 (2019).
9. Tal Z. Zarsky, Incompatible: The GDPR in the Age of Big Data, 47 *Seton Hall L. Rev.* 995, 1012 (2017).
10. Sandra G. Mayson, *Bias In, Bias Out*, 128 Yale L. J. 2218 (2019).
11. Talia B. Gillis, The Input Fallacy, 106 *Minn. L. Rev.* 1175 (2022).
12. Josef Teboho Ansorge, *Identify and Sort: How Digital Power Changed World Politics* (2016).
13. Paul Ohm, Broken Promises of Privacy: Responding to the Surprising Failure of Anonymization, 57 *UCLA L. Rev.* 1701 (2010).
14. Paul M. Schwartz & Daniel J. Solove, The PII Problem: Privacy and a New Concept of Personally Identifiable Information, 86 *N.Y.U. L. Rev.* 1814 (2011).
15. Daniel J. Solove & Woodrow Hartzog, *Breached! Why Data Security Law Fails and How to Improve It* 106–09 (2022).
16. Kashmir Hill, *Your Face Belongs to Us: A Secretive Startup's Quest to End Privacy as We Know It* (2023).
17. *Id.* at 187–88.

18. Solove, *Future of Reputation, supra.*
19. Robert Chesney & Danielle Keats Citron, Deep Fakes: A Looming Challenge for Privacy, Democracy, and National Security, 107 *Cal. L. Rev.* 1753 (2019)
20. Mustafa Suleyman, *The Coming Wave: Technology, Power, and the 21st Century's Greatest Dilemma* 6 (2023).
21. For information about this maxim, see Fred Shapiro, Quotes Uncovered: Forgiveness, Permission, and Awesomeness, Freakonomics [blog] (June 24, 2010), https://freakonomics.com/2010/06/quotes-uncovered-forgiveness-permission-and-awesomeness/.
22. Sarver v. Experian Information Solutions, 390 F.3d 969 (7th Cir. 2004).
23. Daniel J. Solove & Danielle Keats Citron, Risk and Anxiety: A Theory of Data Breach Harms, 96 *Tex. L. Rev.* 737 (2018).
24. TransUnion v. Ramirez, 141 S. Ct. 2190 (2021).
25. 47 U.S.C. § 227.
26. Stoops v. Wells Fargo Bank, 197 F. Supp. 3d 782 (W. D. Pa. 2016).
27. Danielle Keats Citron & Daniel J. Solove, Privacy Harms, 102 *B. U. L. Rev.* 793 (2022).
28. Lauren Henry Scholz, Private Rights of Action in Privacy Regulation, 63 *Wm. & Mary L. Rev.* 1639 (2022).
29. Solove, The Digital Person, *supra.*
30. Daniel J. Solove & Woodrow Hartzog, *Breached! Why Data Security Law Fails and How to Improve It* 106–09 (2022).
31. Citron & Solove, Risk and Anxiety, *supra.*
32. Beck v. McDonald, 949 F.3d 262 (4th Cir. 2017).
33. Solove & Hartzog, *Breached!, supra.*
34. Solove, *Future of Reputation, supra*; Jeff Kosseff, *The United States of Anonymous* (2022).
35. Danielle Keats Citron, *Hate Crimes in Cyberspace* (2014).
36. 47 U.S.C. § 230(c)(1).
37. Zeran v. America Online, Inc., 129 F.3d 327 (4th Cir. 1997).
38. Solove, *Future of Reputation, supra.*
39. *Id.*
40. Citron, *Fight for Privacy, supra*, at xvi; Franks, "Revenge Porn" Reform, *supra.*

Part 3

Privacy and Power

1. Daniel J. Solove, Privacy and Power: Computer Databases and Metaphors for Information Privacy, 53 *Stan. L. Rev.* 1393 (2001).
2. Svyatoslav Biryulin, "Show Me the Incentive and I'll Show You the Outcome," Medium (June 2, 2023), https://medium.com/short-business-articles-by-svya toslav-biryulin/show-me-the-incentive-and-ill-show-you-the-outcome-5343dbb 88df2.
3. Mustafa Suleyman, *The Coming Wave* 5–19 (2023).

The Law's Role

1. Daniel J. Solove & Woodrow Hartzog, The FTC and the New Common Law of Privacy, 114 *Colum. L. Rev.* 583 (2014).
2. Yannis Bakos, Florencia Marotta-Wurgler & David R. Trossen, Does Anyone Read the Fine Print? Consumer Attention to Standard Form Contracts, 43 *J. Legal Stud.* 1 (2014); Omri Ben-Shahar & Adam S. Chilton, Simplification of Privacy Disclosures: An Experimental Test, 45 *J. Legal Stud.* S41, S42 (2016).

3. Woodrow Hartzog & Neil M. Richards, Privacy's Constitutional Moment and the Limits of Data Protection, 61 *B. C. L. Rev.* 1687, 1704 (2020).

4. Florencia Marotta-Wurgler, Will Increased Disclosure Help? Evaluating the Recommendations of the ALI's "Principles of the Law of Software Contracts," 78 *U. Chi. L. Rev.* 165, 168 (2011) (having an "I agree" button next to terms of service only increased readership by 1 percent).

5. Solove, Limitations of Privacy Rights, *supra*; Solove, Murky Consent, *supra*; Neil Richards & Woodrow Hartzog, The Pathologies of Digital Consent, 96 *Wash. U. L. Rev.* 1461, 1476–91 (2019).

6. Daniel J. Solove & Woodrow Hartzog, Kafka in the Age of AI and the Futility of Privacy as Control, 104 *B. U. L. Rev.* 1021 (2024).

7. Robin West, Authority, Autonomy, and Choice: The Role of Consent in the Moral and Political Visions of Franz Kafka and Richard Posner, 99 *Harv. L. Rev.* 384 (1985).

8. Yafit Lev-Aretz & Aileen Nielsen, *Privacy Notice and the Blame Game* 3 (forthcoming, 2025).

9. Daniel J. Solove, Privacy Self-Management and the Consent Dilemma, 126 *Harv. L. Rev.* 1880 (2013).

10. Alessandro Acquisti, Curtis R. Taylor & Liad Wagman, The Economics of Privacy, 54 *J. Econ. Lit.* 442 (2016).

11. Solove, Privacy Self-Management, *supra*.

12. Deborah Blum, *The Poison Squad: One Chemist's Single-Minded Crusade for Food Safety at the Turn of the Twentieth Century* 2, 62–63 (2018).

13. Jessie Singer, *There Are No Accidents: The Deadly Rise of Injury and Disaster—Who Profits and Who Pays the Price* (2022).

14. Daniel J. Solove & Woodrow Hartzog, *Breached! Why Data Security Law Fails and How to Improve It* 106–09 (2022).

How the Law Should Develop

1. 18 U.S.C. § 2710(a)(4).

2. Olmstead v. United States, 277 U.S. 438 (1928).

3. Katz v. United States, 389 U.S. 347 (1967).

4. Daniel J. Solove, *Nothing to Hide: The False Tradeoff Between Privacy and Security* (2011).

5. Daniel J. Solove, Fourth Amendment Pragmatism, 51 *B. C. L. Rev.* 1511 (2010).

6. Daniel J. Solove & Woodrow Hartzog, *Breached! Why Data Security Law Fails and How to Improve It* (2022).

7. Samuel D. Warren & Louis D. Brandeis, The Right to Privacy, 4 *Harv. L. Rev.* 193 (1890).

8. Harry Kalven, Jr., Privacy in Tort Law—Were Warren and Brandeis Wrong?, 31 *L. & Contemp. Probs.* 326, 327 (1966).

9. *Schuyler v. Curtis*, 42 N.E. 22 (N.Y. Ct. App. 1895).

10. *Roberson v. Rochester Folding Box Co.*, 64 N.E. 442 (N.Y. 1902).

11. William L. Prosser, Privacy, 48 *Cal. L. Rev.* 383 (1960).

12. Restatement (Second) of Torts §§ 652A–E (1977).

13. Daniel J. Solove & Neil M. Richards, Prosser's Privacy Law: A Mixed Legacy, 98 *Cal. L. Rev.* 1887 (2010).

14. Olmstead v. United States, 277 U.S. 438 (1928).

15. For a thoughtful discussion of how legal innovation is essential to keep pace with technological innovation, see Joshua A. T. Fairfield, *Runaway Technology: Can Law Keep Up?* 5 (2021).

16. Ari Ezra Waldman, *Industry Unbound: The Inside Story of Privacy, Data, and Corporate Power* (2021).
17. Fairfield, *Runaway Technology, supra* at 5.
18. Chris Jay Hoofnagle, *Federal Trade Commission Privacy Law and Policy* 36 (2016).
19. Daniel J. Solove & Woodrow Hartzog, The FTC and the New Common Law of Privacy, 114 *Colum. L. Rev.* 583, 606–627 (2014).
20. I borrow the term "polycentric" from political scientist and economist Elinor Ostrom. *See* Ostrom, Beyond Markets and States: Polycentric Governance of Complex Economic Systems, 100 *American Econ. Rev.* 641 (2010).

Index

For the benefit of digital users, indexed terms that span two pages (e.g., 52–53) may, on occasion, appear on only one of those pages.

Acquisti, Alessandro, 15, 110, 120 n.10
aggregation effect, 36
Ajunwa, Ifeoma, 115 n.21
algorithmic predictions, 26, 40–42
Allen, Anita, 110
anonymity, 34, 69, 80
appropriation, 3–4, 49
artificial intelligence (AI), 16–17, 33–34, 39, 50
Atwood, Margaret, 2
Auden, W. H., 44

Balkin, Jack, x
Barlow, John Perry, 66
Barocas, Solon, 115 n.21
Bellovin, Steven, 117 n.4
Bentham, Jeremy, 66–67
Bietti, Elettra, 110, 116 n.38
Big Brother, 17–18
Big Data, 34–35, 74
biometric identification, 70–72
black swan, 42
Brandeis, Louis, 29, 95–96, 97–99
Brave New World (Huxley) 2
Brignull, Harry, 61

Calabresi, Guido, 59
California Consumer Privacy Act (CCPA), 88, 117 n.24
Calo, Ryan, 14, 110, 117 n.21
Cardozo, Benjamin, 64
Carpenter v. United States, 36–37
Cavoukian, Ann, 117 n.16
Chander, Anupam, 115 n.21, n.7
Citron, Danielle, 13, 76, 79, 110, 116 n.28, n.29, n.35, 117 n.1
Cohen, Julie, 110, 112 n.5

Communications Decency Act Section 230, 48, 80
COMPAS, 42–43
confidentiality, 61, 63–64
copyright, 31
Corren, Ella, 116 n.42
Crawford, Kate, 16–17, 24
credit reporting, 48, 59–60, 74–75, 77–78
Crootof, Rebecca, 113 n.8, 116 n.25

dark patterns, 61
deepfake images, 68, 73
defamation, 47
Dewey, John, xi–xii, 8–9, 17, 32
digital dossiers, 36
Discrimination, 68–69
Duhigg, Charles, 37
duty of loyalty, 51–52, 64

facial recognition, 71
Fair Credit Reporting Act (FCRA), 48, 75
Fairfield, Joshua, 102, 120 n.15
family resemblances, 3
Federal Trade Commission (FTC), 88, 100–103
Ferguson, Andrew Guthrie, 115 n.2, 118 n.7
fiduciary relationship, 64–65
Foucault, Michel, 66
Fourth Amendment, 36–37, 54
Franks, Mary Anne, 110, 118 n.7, 119 n.40
Freedom of Information Act (FOIA), 35

Gandy, Oscar, 115 n.19, n.9
Geddes, Katrina, 115 n.10

General Data Protection Regulation (GDPR), 1, 44–45, 50, 58, 87, 101–102
Global Positioning System (GPS) data, 36–37
Goffman, Erving, 32
gossip, 29–30, 46–47, 49, 72
Green, Ben, 45

Handmaid's Tale (Atwood), 2
harm, 10, 20, 36–37, 53, 56–57, 68, 73–79, 80–81, 87, 89–93, 105
Hartzog, Woodrow, 56–57, 96, 103, 110, 113 n.8, n.1, n.5, n.2, 114 n.11, 116 n.39, 117 n.3, 118 n.30, n.15, 119 n.30, n.33, n.1, 120 n.3, n.5, n.14
Hill, Kashmir, 118 n.16, n.17
HIPAA (Health Insurance Portability and Accountability Act), 114 n.4
Hoofnagle, Christopher, 110, 117 n.2, 121 n.18
Hurd, Heidi, 49
Huxley, Aldous, 2

identity theft, 70
industrial revolution, 6–7
intellectual property, 31

Joh, Elizabeth, 110, 117 n.8
Johnson, Steven, 56
Jones, Meg Leta, 114 n.6

Kafka, Franz, 2, 18, 89–90
Kahneman, Daniel, 60
Kaminski, Margot, 110, 113 n.8, n.9, n.4, 114 n.7, 116 n.25
Katz v. United States, 117 n.5, 120 n.3
Kim, Nancy, 116 n.44
Kim, Pauline, 115 n.7
Kodak, 29

Lessig, Lawrence, 110, 118 n.2
Loomis, Wisconsin v., 42–43

Maryland, Smith v. 117 n.6
Marotta-Wurgler, Florencia, 110, 116 n.43, 119 n.2, 120 n.4

Matsumi, Hideyuki, 110, 114 n.16, 115 n.1, n.3, n.13
Mayson, Sandra, 68–69, 114 n.8, 115 n.19, n.7
Mechanical Turk, 16
Metaphors, 14–19
Minority Report (movie), 40–41

Nader, Ralph, 63
1984 (Orwell), 2, 17–18
Nissenbaum, Helen, 110, 114 n.5, 117 n.21
notice-and-choice, 49–50, 88
nothing-to-hide argument, 8–10
Nussbaum, Martha, xi

Ohm, Paul, 110, 118 n.13
Olmstead v. United States, 95–96
O'Neil, Cathy, 115 n.12
online social media platforms, 18
Ortega, José y Gasset, 58–59
Orwell, George, 17–18

Panopticon, 66–67
Pasquale, Frank, 110, 116 n.35
privacy
    concept of, 3, 5, 54
    value of, 8–13
privacy notice, 37, 49–51, 53, 63, 87–88, 90, 92
privacy paradox, 20–21, 92
Prosser, William, 98

Quetelet, Lambert Adolphe Jacques, 43–44

reasonable expectation of privacy, 54–55
Reidenberg, Joel, 55
Reporters Committee for Freedom of the Press, DOJ v., 35
Richards, Neil, 66–67, 110, 112 n.1, 113 n.8, n.9, 116 n.39, 118 n.28, n.30, n.31, 120 n.3, n.5, n.13
Right to Privacy (Warren and Brandeis), 29

Samuelson, Pamela, 110
Scholz, Lauren Henry, 110, 118 n.30, 119 n.28
Schwartz, Paul, 66–67, 110, 112 n.5, 118 n.14
Schneier, Bruce, 110, 112 n.7
secrecy paradigm, 30–31, 34–36
security theater, 10
sense enhancement technology, 54–55
Selbst, Andrew, 110, 115 n.21
scraping, 33–34
Smith v. Maryland, 117 n.6
Social Security Number (SSN), 70
Solow-Niederman, Alicia, 114 n.16
Strahilevitz, Lior, 114 n.3
Suleyman, Mustafa, 72–73, 86
Sullivan, Michael, v, 110
Sunstein, Cass, 117 n.21
surveillance, 1–2, 3–4, 9–10, 17–18, 27, 33–34, 54–55, 58, 62, 66–68, 73, 85, 88–89, 94–96
Susser, Daniel, 117 n.21
Swire, Peter, 110

Taleb, Nassim Nicholas, 42
Target, 37
taxonomy of privacy, 4
technology neutrality myth, 24, 38–39, 41–42, 68–69

Telephone Consumer Protection Act (TCPA), 76
third party doctrine, 54
Trial (Kafka), 2, 18
Turow, Joseph, 117 n.2
Tversky, Amos, 60
Twain, Mark, 47
Twitter, 18

Understanding Privacy, 4

Véliz, Carissa, 40–41
Volokh, Eugene, 116 n.31

Wachter, Sandra, 110, 115 n.22
Waldman, Ari, 57, 110, 112 n.1, 113 n.8, 121 n.16
Warren, Samuel, 29, 97–99
Weisberg, Richard, xi
Westin, Alan, x–xi
White, James Boyd, xi
wiretapping, 1, 95–96
Wittgenstein, Ludwig, 3

X (social media platform), 18

Zarsky, Tal, 68, 110
Zittrain, Jonathan, 110